PRAISE FOR C.R.A.S.H.

"Rich is the hardest working person I know! Always personable with people and with spreading positivity to everyone he meets. Onstage, he is the best drummer I have ever played with, hands down. He's one bad dude! Anyone can use this book to inspire their own success!"

> –Jason Aldean
> Multi-Platinum Recording Artist, 3 Time ACM "Entertainer of the Year;" The Most Downloaded male country artist of all time

"*C.R.A.S.H Course for Success* succinctly captures the essence of Rich's success. He is passionate, relentlessly positive, and invested in long term relationships. He energizes every room and gives 100% to everything he does 100% of the time. It's all here in this great read."

> –Jeff Cristee
> Vice President of Global Sales, Cisco

"Neither success nor happiness are ever just an accident . . . but they CAN come by way of a CRASH! Rich's big-hearted stories and time-tested examples show you how to live up to your full potential—and have a GREAT time doing it!"

> –Drew Seeley
> Actor (*Another Cinderella Story, High School Musical, Jersey Boys*)

"This book is a must-read for anyone who needs the validation to jump into the abyss of uncertainty to grab their dream life. Rich's energy had me fired up through the entire book. He's like a freight train in life and has let nothing stand in his way, which is why nothing has. I absolutely love how passionately he conveys his message. This book is motivating, aspiring, and actionable to any entrepreneur or dreamer who's ready to let nothing stand in their way."

> –Melissa Carbone
> Tailgate Fest Founder / CEO
> Ten Thirty One Productions Founder / CEO
> Author of *Ready, Fire, Aim*

"I met Rich years ago on a demanding high-pressure session. Even back then he was a human spark plug, blowing me away with a never let go, make it happen mindset. He was born with dedication, discipline, and desire. You wanna learn how to rock your business? Here's a roadmap."

> –Stan Lynch
> Drummer (Tom Petty and The Heartbreakers), Producer (Don Henley)

"This is an entertaining and fast read from one of the best entertainers in the industry. Rich Redmond has toured, performed, written, and produced with the top names in music today. In *C.R.A.S.H. Course for Success*, he provides great insights into the CRASH framework—Commitment, Relationships, Attitude, Skill, and Hunger—that he uses for top performance and that you can use as well to achieve your full potential."

—Carey Lohrenz
First Female F-14 Tomcat Fighter Pilot in North America
Speaker/Author of Wall Street Journal Best Seller *Fearless Leadership*

"Rich is a natural born motivator and sage. Whenever I need a dose of positive clarity, he is my go-to, and so is this book."

—Skip Williamson
Executive Producer of *Underworld* film franchise
Producer of three #1 films at the US box office
Publisher of *Revolver* magazine

"With CRASH, Rich Redmond has clearly and simply outlined a life path that every hugely successful person I know has followed. I hope Rich's message reaches far and wide because anyone following these simple steps will see huge results."

—Tracy Katsky Boomer
President/Founder of Katco Inc, Executive Producer and Former
Senior VP and Head of Comedy for Fox Broadcasting
Former Senior VP HBO independent productions

"As I've discovered in my own life and through my own teachings, music is a great metaphor to exemplify top performance in all areas of life. Rich does a wonderful job of distilling down complex concepts to their simplest form and helping you, the reader, rock through the learning process by sharing exciting examples from his career in the music business."

—Mark Schulman
Drummer (Pink, Cher, Foreigner)
Motivational Speaker and Author of *Conquering Life's Stage Fright: Three Steps to Top Performance*

"Rich Redmond is one of those people who just pulls you into his positivity! His enthusiasm and joy of life is contagious. He has turned being one of the most 'watched' drummers in the world into a formula for life that is applicable to everyone wanting to squeeze more out of life's orange. This CRASH course will push your reset button and get success in your sights!"

—Devon O'Day
Afternoon Drive Personality 650 AM WSM-Nashville

"After reading Rich's book, I found myself thinking about how beneficial this 'roadmap' would have been in my journey in the movie business. You really can't go wrong using any or all of Rich's principles."
   −Ray Garcia
   Elite Hollywood Key Grip (*The Revenant, Vice, Inception, The Prestige*)

"This book is amazing and insightful. I highly recommended anyone who wants to improve their life to pick up a copy and immerse yourself in it. It's so good!"
   −Robert Channing
   Speed Painter/Mentalist/Speaker *America's Got Talent*

"Unparalleled persistence, preparation, and a passion to please in every relationship is the fuel for Rich's success. He shares these insights with the reader using real, pragmatic, down-to-earth, insightful stories. If you put the time into reading this book, you will learn how to CRASH into success in your life, and you will live with no regrets!"
   −Glenn Rupert
   World renowned Speaker and Consultant
   Vice-President, The Rupert Group, Inc.

"Rich Redmond is a great friend and mentor. His book will motivate you, excite you, and inspire you to achieve YOUR goals in life!"
   −Cole Marcus
   Drummer/Winner of "America's Most Talented Kid"
   Actor in *I Can Only Imagine*

"The minute I met Rich Redmond I immediately connected with him. His passion, his energy, and his enthusiasm about how one catalyst can make a significant difference in another person's life was contagious. Rich has spent his lifetime cultivating this course, honing it, refining it, and perfecting it. This book is a guide to experiencing an uncommon life and I highly recommend it to everyone."
   −Coach Micheal Burt
   The Super Coach
   13-time bestselling author
   Creator of Monster Producer

"I felt so empowered after reading this book. My personal mantra is 'Dream Big or Don't Bother.' Imagine what will be in my future using CRASH with focus and intention."
   −Jerilynn Stephens
   Emmy Nominated & Guild Award Winning Celebrity Hairstylist

"Rich has that rare ability to transform his real-life experiences as a world-class drummer to best business practices and artfully create a tool kit that questions, challenges, and provokes the reader to be the best they can be. Literally filled with REAL road-tested advice, CRASH will guide you to produce the results you want."
    —Freddie Ravel
    Keynote Maestro, Grammy Performer, and Business Speaker

"CRASH is a tremendous program that will take you and your team to a higher level! This framework for success is built upon key concepts that harness the power of the human spirit to drive optimal performance across your entire organization. Rich delivers CRASH through a mix of energy, passion, and experiences. If you want to lead from the front . . . check out Rich's story."
    —John Moses
    Vice President of Sales, Cisco

"Rich's message resonates with not just one gold nugget but the whole rock! His energy is always moving and seeking the last seats in the room, and his book does the same from chapter to chapter. You feel his excitement and commitment to his *CRASH! Course for Success*. Thank you, Rich, for sharing the roadmap and tools to navigate a path to success."
    —Christine Hilgert, CMP
    Senior Vice President, Meeting Expectations

"*C.R.A.S.H. Course for Success* is a great read! It shows how anyone can use his C.R.A.S.H principles in their personal life and business life to reach their full potential. So entertaining and engaging!"
    —Nathan Jamail
    Expert Leader and author of the best-selling *The Leadership Playbook*

C.R.A.S.H.

COURSE FOR

SUCCESS

C.R.A.S.H.

COURSE FOR SUCCESS

5 WAYS TO SUPERCHARGE YOUR PERSONAL AND PROFESSIONAL LIFE

RICH REDMOND

WITH PAUL DEEPAN

A CRASH ENTERTAINMENT PUBLICATION

CRASH! Course for Success:
5 Ways to Supercharge Your Personal and Professional Life

Copyright © 2019 Rich Redmond

Foreword © 2019 Jeff Cristee

This is a work of narrative nonfiction. The author has tried to recreate events, locales, and conversations from his memories of them. Any errors are unintentional.

Editing by Stars and Stone Books
Cover Design by Carrie Miller
Author and Cover Photograph Chris and Todd Owyoung

A Production of Crash Entertainment
crashforsuccess.com

Digital Edition 1.0
Print Edition 0

Print ISBN: 9781733757003
Digital ISBN: 9781733757010

FOREWORD
BY JEFF CRISTEE

Jeff Cristee with My Drumsticks

A s the leader of a large sales team for a Global 100 technology company exiting the recession in 2013, I had just been through one of the toughest stretches of business our industry had ever seen. After several staff reductions, I received the green light to get my team of approximately fifty sales and engineering managers together for an offsite meeting. This was to be one of the most important meetings I would ever run as a leader. We were in desperate need of a fresh approach. I knew the session needed to be educational but fun.

Rich's "CRASH! Course for Success" had that special mix of inspiration and high-energy entertainment, and it was the perfect program to kick off our meeting. Instead of choosing a dull conference room with power points and projectors, we had our team meet at midday in the legendary Ghost Bar, over fifty stories above the Las Vegas Strip.

We quickly learned that nothing happens without the drummer. The drummer is the leader of any musical group and every organization in the world needs a great leader. It all starts with a countdown to excellence. '1-2-3 BAM!' There was no mistaking the meeting had started as Rich pummeled his drums with passionate force. Rich whipped his drums into submission as the entire room was mesmerized by his unwavering youthful energy. This was a man possessed!

Rich charismatically engaged the audience and highlighted his CRASH! Principals for Success. Commitment! Relationships! Attitude! Skill! Hunger! Easy to remember and easy to incorporate into your life . . . no matter how old you are or what career path you are on. Rich had my team captivated with personal stories, epic music, primal drumming, and unforgettable educational takeaways. We had members of the audience joining him to play drums and even sing. Rich treated everyone like a rockstar! Rich was passion personified. We emerged from the session with renewed commitment to be the best sales organization in our industry. There was education. There was inspiration. There was motivation. There was sweat! If my team could approach their job with a tenth of Rich's passion, I knew we could rewrite the rulebooks. The session with Rich was the perfect way to get us to think differently and embrace a fresh approach.

I was so blown away by Rich that I asked him to join us for our Global Sales meeting a year later at Caesars' Palace in Las Vegas. I hosted this event for nearly eight hundred new sales personnel from across the globe. Again, Rich captured the entire room's attention like a seasoned snake charmer. His message connected with everyone and transcended age gaps and cultural barriers. Rich's enthusiasm for his craft, for his message, and for *life* simply cannot be ignored. Rich reminded everyone what it takes to be your best every day. This was the perfect kick off for a great week at our Global Sales Meeting.

Jeff Cristee at My Drum Set

Since this time, Rich has done many more events for our teams and I have gotten to know him very well personally. CRASH! is not only his approach to success, but also his approach to life. He is a committed, relationship-driven, skilled, and talented speaker whose reputation proceeds him. Rich wears a positive attitude like a badge of honor and through it all remains hungry for new challenges and experiences. I will surely share this book with friends and colleagues alike and look forward to seeing what other amazing things Rich creates in his life! No matter what, I am certain that Rich will continue to change the lives of all he comes in contact with.

Jeff Cristee
Vice President
Worldwide Sales Training
Cisco Systems

INTRODUCTION TO C.R.A.S.H.

> IF THEY CAN MAKE PENICILLIN OUT OF MOLDY
> BREAD, THEY CAN MAKE SOMETHING OUT OF
> YOU.
>
> —MUHAMMAD ALI

Welcome!

Hello! As a professional drummer for over 30 years, I've been able to hear myself on the radio, see myself on television, and play sold-out shows in some of the world's most iconic venues. I have toured, recorded, and/or performed with: Jason Aldean, Garth Brooks, Ludacris, Kelly Clarkson, Bryan Adams, Bob Seger, Chris Cornell, Joe Perry, Jewel, Miranda Lambert, Keith Urban, Dolly Parton, Derek Trucks, Chris Stapleton, Florida Georgia Line and many others.

I've recorded drums and percussion on twenty-six #1 singles with sales well over the twenty million mark. You can even hear me on the radio every day, around the clock, with a reach of one billion ears. As a high-energy live showman, I perform sold out shows nightly in amphitheaters, arenas, and stadiums across the world, reaching over two million fans per year. Some of these venues include Madison Square Garden, The Hollywood Bowl, Fenway Park, Wrigley Field, Red Rocks, The Gorge, The Rose Bowl, Levi Stadium, Gillette Stadium, and countless NFL stadium and MLB parks.

I've appeared multiple times on television shows such as *Saturday Night Live*, *The Voice*, *American Idol*, The Grammy Awards, *The Tonight Show* (with Leno, O'Brien, and Fallon), *The Today Show*, Conan O'Brien, Jimmy Kimmel, Craig Ferguson, *Good Morning America*, *Ellen*, The CMA Awards, ACM Awards, CMT Awards, and ACA Awards, as well as being prominently featured in twenty popular music videos. I've produced three #1 hits for the groups Thompson Square and Parmalee.

As a songwriter, I've celebrated three #1 songs with Australia's The Wolfe Brothers.

As the touring and recording drummer with Jason Aldean, I've been a part of changing the sound of modern country rock music. Jason is the three-time Academy of Country Music "Entertainer of The Year" and the most downloaded male country artist of all time. To have been part of this journey, playing every state in the U.S. and sixteen other countries, is an incredible feeling.

To top it all off, I was named "Country Drummer of The Year" in *Modern Drummer Magazine* (the most prestigious drum publication in the world) in 2010, 2015, 2016, 2017, and 2018.I played in the prestigious 1:00 Lab Band at The University of North Texas and received my Master's Degree in Music Education.

I combined my academic training and real-life experiences with the heart of a teacher to bring my "CRASH! Course for Success" motivational drumming to corporate events around the world. Some of my clients include: Cisco, Johnson and Johnson, Hewlett-Packard, Microsoft, Alestra, Tri-Star Healthcare, Amerifirst Financial, Adtran, Unified Bank, The Grammy Camp, and many others.

So why do I share all of this with you? Through hard work and persistence, I achieved the dreams of my youth. I want everyone to accomplish their dreams in life just like I did, and that is why I created this system for success, called CRASH!

CRASH! is an easy-to-remember acronym that stands for:

The CRASH! Elements

CRASH! can work for anyone from children to adults, and will allow you to create success in your personal and professional life.

I use a talk-play-talk-play format when presenting my CRASH! concept to audiences, but real life isn't that methodical or streamlined. So, in addition to talking about each element on its own, I also show how the CRASH! elements interconnect by sharing stories of how I applied CRASH! in different periods of my own life. You can use my life as a model for how these concepts will help you achieve your own dreams.

SUCCESS IS NEVER GUARANTEED

A View of Success from My Perspective

Following the CRASH! formula will not *guarantee* your success in life, but I do believe that following the formula will stack the odds in your favor. Conversely, *not* following it will deprive you of a proven road map for success.

In my experience, people who show unshakeable Commitment to their dreams, their craft, and their Relationships while maintaining a positive Attitude and rejecting complacency are the ones who tend to be "lucky" enough to be in the right place at the right time.

While luck, God, or your version of a higher power will influence how your life unfolds, *you* play a huge role. You have a lot more power than you think. You will also have to work harder than you imagine. There's a saying that's been around for a long time: "The harder you work, the luckier you get." Variations on this saying have been attributed to Thomas Jefferson, Steven Leacock, Samuel Goldwyn, and others. The CRASH! formula gives you a method for working hard, executing your plans effectively, and transforming your life.

DESTINATION SUCCESS

Imagine that you are the driver of a car starting a journey toward a destination called Success. What if you had a system that would:

- Give you a road map to that destination
- Teach you how to fine-tune your car to optimize its performance
- Help you figure out the type of fuel you are using and where to find it
- Guide you to become a better driver during the actual race
- Encourage you to relate to the other drivers to help them become successful

---

CRASH! puts you in the driver's seat of the car and gives you the most important tools you'll need to arrive at Destination Success. Trees may fall across the road, other drivers may cut you off, and you may run out of gas, but CRASH! keeps you on track to your destination.

I'm proud that my successes in life did not come at the expense of others. Instead, I've tried to help others to become successful in their own pursuits. Many great people have helped me along the way. No man is an island. Everyone needs help from their friends.

Success is *not* a zero-sum game; successful people have an obligation to support others. An explicit piece of the CRASH! formula is Relationships and how you treat other people. You should always strive to assist others. It's incredibly fun for me to help someone achieve their dreams.

HOW DO YOU DEFINE SUCCESS?

The beauty of CRASH! is that it offers an intentional road

map to achieve any goal. You don't have to be a drummer to use CRASH! You can be a writer, chef, athlete, actor, soccer mom, or businessperson: the CRASH! formula will work for you. If you structure your thinking, habits, and behaviors around the CRASH! framework, you will develop a life system that will move you quickly toward your desired destination.

Everyone defines success differently. Some people define success by what others can see, like material possessions or achievement in their fields. Others may focus more on internal benchmarks, such as developing quality Relationships or spiritual growth.

I wanted to become a top-call, touring and recording drummer in Nashville. This was a very specific goal that I was able to achieve. The more people asked me how I did it, the more I realized that I had an opportunity to help others by telling my story.

No matter what your goals are, CRASH! can help you achieve them!

- Do you want to go to medical school? CRASH!
- Do you want to eat healthier and lose weight? CRASH!
- Do you want to do compete in an Ironman Triathlon? CRASH!
- Do you want to repair a Relationship? CRASH!
- Do you want to be a top performer in your company? CRASH!
- Do you want to start your own business and see it thrive? CRASH!

Use this book as a roadmap to *your* success!

CRASH! CHALLENGE QUESTIONS

1. What are some of your goals for life? Write them down.
2. Who has helped you in your journey to success? Call them and thank them immediately!
3. Are you helping others to achieve their dreams? Who could you be helping right now?

CHAPTER 1
COMMITMENT

NOTHING IN THE WORLD CAN TAKE THE PLACE OF
PERSISTENCE. TALENT WILL NOT: NOTHING IS MORE
COMMON THAN UNSUCCESSFUL MEN WITH TALENT.
GENIUS WILL NOT: UNREWARDED GENIUS IS ALMOST
A PROVERB. EDUCATION ALONE WILL NOT: THE
WORLD IS FULL OF EDUCATED DERELICTS.
PERSISTENCE AND DETERMINATION ALONE ARE
OMNIPOTENT.

-CALVIN COOLIDGE

Working My Craft

hat does it take to be a successful musician, dancer, or painter? How about a successful salesperson, manager, or entrepreneur? How about a successful athlete or life partner? The answer: Commitment.

Commitment is the first word in the CRASH! acronym for a reason. Commitment can be defined as a "pledge or undertaking" or "to be dedicated to something." Anyone who has enjoyed staying power in business will tell you that a massive amount of dedication is required to succeed. All vocations are competitive, and every industry is tough as nails. Playing sports takes a tremendous amount of dedication. So does becoming a great salesperson, navigating a long-term Relationship, or starting your own business. The undeniable truth is, Commitment is universally important for success, no matter how you define it.

SIGNS OF A LACK OF COMMITMENT

- An employee who never goes the extra mile
- A talented student who only does the bare minimum
- A romantic partner who gives priority to anything but the relationship

During my career I've seen musicians of all ages and levels of ability perform. Great musicians fuse technique and passion at the highest level. But I've also noticed that a disappointing number of musicians lack Commitment in their performance. If you've seen a musician play with low energy or a lifeless style, you may not have been able to put your finger on why, but I bet you thought their playing lacked drive, or that special It factor. They didn't seem fully engaged or present in the moment, and consequently they couldn't help you experience the music's full potential. When I play, I try to be larger than life. I send my energy to the people sitting in the farthest seats in the house.

No matter what field you are in, people can tell if you are authentically committed to what you are doing.

Sending Energy to the Back Rows

SHOW UP!

Commitment is about showing up and being prepared to perform. Showing up, both physically and mentally, will put you ahead of everyone else. I've played dehydrated, jet-lagged, sleep deprived, and sick with the flu. You know what they say in show biz: the show must go on.

When prepping for a CRASH! speaking engagement, I learn everything I can about the host company's corporate culture, products or services, and which members of their team will be in the audience. The same type of preparation is needed for any live musical performance. Long before they've arrived on stage, a committed group of musicians will have spent hours and hours of preparation both individually and collectively to create that special experience for the audience.

Commitment is critically important in business as well. Let's use a sales rep as an example. A great salesperson researches the market to discover potential problems and knows the benefits and limitations of their product or service, and they know how it can best serve a client.

Just as in music, the time spent in front of your client (performing) ends up being a very small part of the actual time you invest in becoming successful in your career.

I could easily draw similar examples for teachers, athletes, doctors, retail workers, hospitality workers, bank tellers, corporate employees—anyone from the CEO of a Fortune 500 company to the newest hire or intern—or a whole host of other vocations. It's very clear that Commitment is vital. Without Commitment, any success is accidental.

Doing a Soundcheck Before a Performance in 2008

ASK THE RIGHT QUESTIONS

When I play drums, I'm constantly asking myself questions. Am I balancing the dynamics between my limbs? Am I using proper tone and articulation? Am I listening to the other musicians and making it easy for the whole band to play together? Am I making the music feel good? These are very important questions every musician should ask.

UNIVERSAL QUESTIONS

- Am I performing my tasks efficiently, accurately, and to the best of my abilities?
- What are the real problems or concerns of the person I'm working with/helping/selling to?
- Can I authentically help solve this problem using my product/service/expertise/training?
- Have I asked the right questions and uncovered the right information?
- What obstacles are in the way of me performing my task for or with this person? How can I get around the obstacles or remove them so we can work as a team?
- Are we ready to take the next step, whatever that may be?

If you have a natural talent in areas such as music, sports, business, or any creative endeavor, and have gone on to excel in your field, you have demonstrated a Commitment to craft that helped you turn natural ability into expertise.

These techniques can be put to work by anyone, at any age, in any field.

BE PREPARED FOR OPPORTUNITIES

REPETITION IS THE MOTHER OF LEARNING, THE FATHER OF ACTION, WHICH MAKES IT THE ARCHITECT OF ACCOMPLISHMENT.

-ZIG ZIGLAR

Becoming committed to your craft means being prepared for any opportunity that comes your way. In any arena, preparation always includes the repetitive practice of tasks, action steps, or drills until they become second nature. Without this constant practice, true expertise in any field is never attained.

Musicians practice scale after scale and exercise after exercise until they become part of their DNA. Soldiers assemble and disassemble their weapons until they can do it blindfolded. Hockey players shoot puck after puck at nets, basketball players shoot ball after ball at hoops. Sales people and speakers practice presentation after presentation until they hear them in their sleep. Surgeons do procedure after procedure, internists see patient after patient. Chefs cook meal after meal, teachers give class after class, artists draw line after line. Writers write sentence upon sentence . . . Commitment takes many forms.

RADICAL COMMITMENT

> THOUGH YOU CAN LOVE WHAT YOU DO NOT
> MASTER, YOU CANNOT MASTER WHAT YOU DO
> NOT LOVE.
>
> > —MOKOKOMA MOKHONOANA

THREE SIGNS OF RADICAL COMMITMENT

- Your skills, talents, and personality are a good fit for whatever you're doing.
- You come alive, so that your actions feed your heart, your soul, or some other intangible besides your wallet.
- You want to do this thing, possibly every day for the rest of your life.

Unless all three of these dimensions are met, it will be difficult for you to maintain a high level of Commitment.

ENJOY IT!

Talk show host David Letterman once asked the late Warren Zevon if he had any advice for people as he was approaching his final days. He said, "Enjoy every sandwich." Those words resonated with me. We only have so much time on Earth and life can be taken away at any moment. Don't wait until you are old to think this way. I told myself very early on in my career that I would always play at 100% of my ability, inspire others, and make it a fun experience. If you think and act this way, the doors of opportunity will forever swing open for you.

Even if you're good at something, you still have to practice. If you have a natural aptitude but don't enjoy the process, you won't Commit to practicing, and you will never become an expert.

HEALTH RISK!

I practiced rim shots on my snare drum so much as a young man. I would take my marching drum and play for hours in my garage, attempting to never miss that magical placement of drumstick on the head and rim of the drum. I loved that sound and practiced it so much that it became part of my being.

To achieve this technique consistently, I set my snare drum up in a way that made me strike a portion of my upper quadricep. After doing this for thirty years, I now have no hair that grows on my leg. My commitment manifested in a physical way on my body. That is *radical* commitment!

During my 2018 touring season, my doctor informed me that I had a profound inguinal hernia (so that's what the bump is?). He urged me to seek surgery immediately, but said that it would be a four-week recovery. With my demanding tour schedule with Jason Aldean, I just didn't have the time to recover. We had the big tour supporting the *Rearview Town* record, and my band needed me. They didn't want another drummer on stage with them; when you spend eighteen years together, you get very used to each other and comfortable.

I put off the surgery until the end of the year, after the tour. Playing the drums is so physical and my doctor told me that at any moment on stage, I could require emergency surgery and it would be painful. I literally put my own health at risk for the sake of my band. That's *radical* commitment.

PRACTICE IT!

I know a young man who, as a little boy, could zip a wicked baseball into your glove with amazing precision, throw a football with a perfect spiral, and shoot a promising slap shot on the ice. His parents had dollar signs dancing in their eyes, imagining future athletic scholarships to a world-class university.

One problem: the kid hated sports! He *hated* the way his wet hockey equipment stuck to his body after practice. He thought baseball was completely boring and football was just plain stupid.

Despite his natural athletic ability, sports left him cold. He would never Commit to them because he didn't enjoy them. His parents wisely spent their time, money, and resources to help him develop Skills that he truly loved.

Ultimately, he thrived in his field because it was the right fit for him.

HAVE A GOAL . . . AND A PLAN

A GOAL WITHOUT A DEADLINE IS JUST A DREAM.

                                              -ANONYMOUS

Commitment also means knowing where you want to go, creating a plan for how to get there, and having an idea for how long it could take. Plans and goals can change, but you need to have a plan to start with.

A life without goals will leave you wandering aimlessly, without direction.

Dreams Come True

When I arrived in Nashville, my goal was to become a top-call touring and session drummer. I achieved that goal years ago, but I still work hard every day to maintain it. Like many musicians, I survived hard times by waiting tables, doing construction work, and substitute teaching.

I hit roadblocks, doors were slammed in my face, and I heard the word "no" a million times. But I had a vision for my future and a laser focus.

I fell in love with rejection. Every "no" felt like a step closer to my destination. I could have packed my bags and quit, but I didn't because I had two things: my dream, and my Commitment to see it through.

TELL THE WORLD YOUR PLAN

> WHATEVER THE MIND CAN CONCEIVE AND BELIEVE, IT CAN ACHIEVE.
>
> -NAPOLEON HILL

Commit to your beliefs and goals and shout that Commitment from a mountaintop. Have the courage to dream big, and then make yourself accountable to your goals. Stand by your words and let the world see your beliefs though your actions.

If you fuel your Commitment with conviction, passion, and persistence, you will see your dreams become a reality. If you've got the talent and the Commitment to work hard, and if you believe you deserve success, then you have what it takes to grab your dreams and make them come true.

I've been playing the drums every day of my life for over forty years. Making music defines me as a human being. It's truly how I express myself. Knowing that I get to pursue my passion gets me out of bed every day.

Successful people will say the same thing about what they do. For instance, I'm absolutely certain that legendary investor Warren Buffett loves finding amazing investment opportunities. I'm sure that Denzel Washington loves signing on to a new project with a great script, and that Stephen King gets a thrill out of coming up with inventive ways to scare millions of readers. I bet Steve Jobs must have been ecstatic when he created a revolutionary product that would change the technological landscape.

Have the courage to set yourself apart. Doing what everyone else has done helps you learn your craft in the beginning, but eventually you will need to find your own voice. It's been said in the music business that good composers borrow, but great composers steal. Use successful people as a model for your own journey by stealing the methods that worked for them. Because everyone is unique, those "stolen" ideas will be transformed into something only you could have created. Then you'll be one step closer to setting yourself apart from the pack.

CREATE SOMETHING NEW

ADAPT WHAT IS USEFUL, REJECT WHAT IS USELESS, AND ADD WHAT IS SPECIFICALLY YOUR OWN.

-BRUCE LEE

Bruce Lee was arguably the greatest kung fu artist who ever lived. But after he mastered every style of kung fu, he created his own "formless" style that allowed him to be creative in the moment and beat his opponents. Anyone can learn from Bruce Lee. He started with what was known, Committed to learning everything possible, and then invented something brand new.

His Commitment gave him a competitive edge, and you can do the same. How can you be the Bruce Lee of your business?

CRASH! CHALLENGE QUESTIONS

1. How are you committed to yourself?
2. How are you committed to your organization?
3. Have you defined your goals and written them down? Do that now.
4. What are your specific plans to achieve those goals? Write them down.
5. What is your exact timeline to complete those goals? Write it down.

CHAPTER 2
RELATIONSHIPS

NO MAN IS AN ISLAND.

-JOHN DONNE

*With Jason Aldean and My Bandmates
at Madison Square Garden, 2012*

Nobody gets to the top by themselves. People that believe in you help you along the way. But how do you *allow* people to help you? Relationships.

Zig Ziglar once said: "If people like you, they'll listen to you, but if they trust you, they'll do business with you." For you to make a sale or land a job, people have to know you, like you, and trust you.

Allowing people to know you comes first. You have to

let them see what kind of person you are. When I first came to Nashville, no one knew me. I was starting over. I needed visibility, so I went out every night, shaking hands and forming alliances. I needed musicians to like me, listen to me, and trust me. Once they trusted me, I could build professional Relationships and eventually form a team of collaborators who shared mutual trust, respect, and admiration.

LIKEABILITY

Highly successful people tend to be authentic, secure, and sincere. Being genuinely likeable is paramount.

Smart organizations and smart individuals understand this concept. Take, for example, the New Zealand All Blacks national rugby team, arguably the most successful sports franchise in the world. New Zealand's win-rate over the last hundred years in international play is over 75%. It's a phenomenal record, and an achievement matched by no other elite team in any sport.

But in 2004, something was wrong. The 2003 World Cup had gone badly, and by the start of the following year, senior All Blacks began threatening to leave. Team discipline was suffering, and, worst of all, the All Blacks were losing.

In response, a new management team began to rebuild the team from the inside out. The goal was a fresh culture that placed emphasis on individual character and personal leadership. Their mantra? "Better People Make Better All Blacks." The result? From 2005 to 2013, the All Blacks had an incredible win-rate of just over 86%, and another Rugby

World Cup.

One of the concepts that informed their new principles was the Maori word *Whanau*. Whanau is the belief that helping others helps yourself, and that focusing on other people's needs is more important than your own. When they rebuilt their team, they looked for more than just talent in their players. They needed athletes with *character*. You can develop talent, but you cannot change character.

Jason Aldean's Band: Jay Jackson, Jack Sizemore, Me, Kurt Allison, and Tully Kennedy Backstage at The Tonight Show

Many bands break up because of individual members' character flaws. Bands that stand the test of time are made up of like-minded individuals committed to a common goal. This is the case for Jason Aldean and his band. Jason, Kurt Allison, Tully Kennedy, and I have been playing together for nearly twenty years, mostly because we all like and respect each other. We are still together because we are a group of friends who always puts the success of the music and the band before our own egos. Jack Sizemore and Jay Jackson joined the band in 2010.

Treat everyone with respect and compassion, and allow them to be surprised by your sincerity, generosity, and kindness. After all, no one person is better than anyone else.

POSITIVE AND NEGATIVE

With These Kinds of People in Your Life,
You'll Always Be Having Fun

There is no law of Relationships that says you have to hang out with negative people. Remember this: birds of a feather flock together. Surround yourself with positive people who feel and act like you do. Strive to create sincere, lifelong, mutually beneficial Relationships with like-minded people.

Successful Relationships are formed when you give to others. Always think about what you can do to help the other person first. The most certain method to earn respect and trust is to be genuinely interested in helping other people.

Let's say an opportunity comes along that you aren't interested in, but that you know is perfect for a someone in your network. Give that person the chance for a huge break and refer them instead.

Countless times in my career I've connected friends and musicians with life-changing opportunities. I see this as my responsibility as a successful person. I use my network as a tool to help my community and to affect people positively, because that's my life's purpose. Paying opportunity forward in this manner is one of the surest paths to insure *you* will be helped in the future.

HOW TO EARN TRUST

> IT IS MUTUAL TRUST, EVEN MORE THAN MUTUAL INTEREST, THAT HOLDS HUMAN ASSOCIATIONS TOGETHER.
>
> -H. L. MENCKEN

Those that hire us to perform a specific task assume that we can deliver the Skills for our job. I pride myself on being a highly trained drummer who can authentically and enthusiastically cover vast musical ground. I have experience playing jazz, big band, classical, rock, fusion, funk, country, pop, reggae, R&B, and Latin styles. It took copious time, focus, and follow-through to achieve this versatility. This versatility was a goal of mine so that I could (and do) play with anyone in the world. When people hire me, they trust that I have this highly developed Skill set.

Excellence draws opportunities to you.

> - What does versatility look like in your field?
> - What steps are you taking to achieve it?

TRUST BECOMES RECOMMENDATION

It's important to create lifelong fans. Our band has worked hard for years to create a loyal fanbase. Similarly, corporations work to create products that will inspire brand loyalty.

I will go out of my way to find my preferred brand of coffee, even risking missing my flight to find them in an airport. This company hires "people people," who greet me with a smile and ask for my name. The company's culture and products give me a positive experience, and I am now a lifelong customer.

I always keep that in mind with my drumming. I strive to create an amazing experience for my fans, from the people who come to a show to someone who drives five hours to attend one of my drum clinics.

Every business interaction is an opportunity to deepen relationships, and every social event is a chance to foster opportunities. I am still doing business with people I met thirty years ago. I always make it a point to mix business and pleasure.

Filling the Room with Energy During an Event

In all of my years of drumming, I have only gotten *one* job from an audition. But even that was mostly a formality because the drummer leaving strongly recommended me. He vouched for my Skills and my ability to interact with others. He left a message on management's voicemail that went like this:

"You guys can have your audition, but I promise you: Rich is the guy. He is a team player who always shows up prepared and on time. He's a versatile musician who can take direction, and he has a good personality."

Every other job I have gotten in my long career has come from a recommendation. That is the power of Relationships. People have to know, like, and trust you. The people who recommend me know they can stick their necks out and champion me. They know that I will deliver on the bandstand, be a team player, and get along with the other musicians on and off stage. They know I won't damage their credibility by being unprepared or difficult.

Similarly, when someone sticks their neck out for you, you are *required* to knock it out of the park.

Relationships make the world go 'round, especially if they are based on mutual respect, trust, and sincerity. Building authentic Relationships takes a *lot* of time and effort. If you are willing to commit to this, you will set yourself apart.

Varied Relationships Lead to New Opportunities, Such as Producing a Video Series (Drumming in the Modern World)

My Relationships are varied and plentiful. They include songwriters, producers, artists, managers, booking agents, publishers, studio owners, club owners, and more. I've made a point of getting to know people working in every area of the music industry: touring, recording, merchandising, publishing, and others.

I typically see all of the same camera operators and stage personnel on every TV show I record. Whether it's The Grammys, The ACM Awards, The CMA Awards, The CMT Awards, *Good Morning America*, *The Today Show*, *The*

Tonight Show with Jimmie Fallon, or *Jimmy Kimmel,* it's all the same faces.

With Cameraman Jamey Tidwell at the Houston Rodeo

People in every industry have cliques and networks. People champion people. I make it a point to keep in touch with all of these fine folks because I know I will see them year after year. I always make sure that I am personable and easy to work with. I try to make *their* job easier. Remember that you will always see the same faces on the way up that you will on the way down, so treat people kindly and value their relationships.

Also, why limit yourself or your social circle to one small group? By associating with many circles, your next job can come from anyone at any time. It really is a small world, and many of the gatekeepers know each other. This is true for all vocations, not just music. As I expand my business interests, I am asking everyone I know to recommend me to film and TV directors, casting directors, acting coaches, event planners, speakers' bureaus, and fellow authors, to name just a few.

The most important part of those Relationships is actually meeting and spending time with people. I'm often asked by struggling musicians via social media platforms to 'keep them in mind' for major auditions. It's not that I don't want to help, but how could I champion someone when I don't know them personally? More than that, I don't know anything about their playing, personality, or people Skills. This really is an unrealistic request.

Many of the musicians who message me live outside the major music areas of New York, Los Angeles, and Nashville. In my industry, there are thousands of qualified musicians in the larger markets scratching and clawing for the available work, so there is never a need to look outside of those cities. You have to go to the mountain; it will *not* come to you. As is true of many businesses, location is everything. One of the most important things you can do to realize success is to move to where your Skill set is in demand and start cultivating sincere, lasting Relationships. You must be present to win, and yet I find that most people are unwilling to go where the opportunities are. If you are willing to relocate, you will automatically set yourself apart from your competition.

> - Are you willing to go where the action is?
> - Are you willing to relocate to change your life for the better?

RELATIONSHIPS WITH YOUR TEAM

Being comfortable with the people on your team is paramount. I am fortunate that I have been touring for so many years with my best friends. We know each other inside and out, and many times we know what is going to happen musically long before it does. We anticipate, we encourage, and we listen. There is a brotherhood and a Commitment to make our show sound, look, and feel great. There must be a culture of trust and support for any team to be highly effective.

Relationships are everything.

Team Aldean in LA

CRASH! CHALLENGE QUESTIONS

1. How are you cultivating your current Relationships?
2. How could you be fostering new Relationships for future growth and development?
3. Who really has your back? Write down their names.
4. Who has helped you get where you are? Write down their names.
5. Pick up the phone and call them—right now!

CHAPTER 3
ATTITUDE

Share a Smile Everywhere You Go

No matter who you are or what you do, Attitude is everything. I have never met a single person on this earth who wants to communicate on even a surface level with someone who oozes negativity. A musician can spend years developing flawless technique, speed, and power and never share the stage with other musicians because of a horrible Attitude. Conversely, if you make it to the big stage, a bad Attitude can take away that privilege just as fast. Attitude will make or break you!

You can park a luxury car outside and walk into a room wearing the best clothes and the most expensive accessories, and people might be momentarily impressed. But what people will remember is how you made them feel and the experience you have together. Attitude is the *one* thing people will always remember about you, without fail. It is the most important factor in determining the shape of your life.

Did you know it takes almost twice as much energy to generate a negative thought as it does a positive thought? Why work so hard? Develop the habit of staying positive, and let your team-player spirit shine. People will be attracted to your energy and you'll be able to pursue your major purpose in life every day.

> • What is your purpose? If you haven't already, write it down.

THE POWER OF POSITIVITY

I was attracted to the idea of positivity at a very young age. My mother collected books by authors who wrote about the power of the mind and about how our thoughts could become things. I absorbed many compelling lessons from those books that still influence me today. Thanks, Mom!

"Change your mind, change your life" is a fantastic thought process that I have brought to my own career with great results. I believe people from all walks of life are subliminally attracted to others with great Attitudes.

Therefore, you can set yourself apart from the pack by wielding a winning Attitude like a sword.

There are many people across the globe that possess a high-level Skill set for their occupation, but that do not have the kind of positive Attitude that makes people want to work with them consistently. Employees who are constantly upbeat and optimistic will always find work. The ones that aren't simply don't work as much.

Enthusiasm Is Contagious

We must consistently exceed expectations and deliver the goods with smiles on our faces. Your Skills may get you in the door, but it's your Attitude that will keep you there. Be enthusiastic! Enthusiasm is contagious, and I have used it as a tool to shift destructive and unproductive environments into positive, productive workplaces.

I recommend living in the land of unicorns and rainbows—I do. When I play, I'm hoping my employers will notice my positive Attitude as much as my playing and will want to call me again. All businesses thrive on repeat customers. Focus on giving more than receiving, and you will always be in demand.

LEAVE IT AT HOME

In 2011, our band played the Hollywood Bowl. It was a magical show that had sold out in an hour. All the true believers in Los Angeles were there, packed into the Bowl's twelve thousand seats. I had a massive argument with my (now) ex-wife earlier that day. I asked myself, why did this have to happen on a day this special? But I let go of all my negative emotions for those two hours and played a flawless, heartfelt show steeped in energy, excitement, and musicianship. I couldn't let my personal life interfere with my work responsibilities. My band and those twelve thousand fans were counting on me, and I gave them my all. I exceeded their expectations and I was able to proudly look at myself in the mirror afterwards. We can't let negativity creep into our workspace. Frankly, most of our employers don't care what's happening in our personal life. Most of them simply want your best at all times. If you're on the payroll, then you have to "bring it." You have to develop the ability to flip that switch and go into performance mode, no matter what line of work you are in.

A top-notch producer friend of mine called me a few years ago to record drums on a project for a band. In the music industry, it has become increasingly popular for musicians to record their parts individually, away from the rest of the band. But for this session, my friend wanted us to all record in the same room at the same time.

He knew from hiring me in the past that I'd stay positive

for one take or fifteen takes, and that my high energy level would positively affect the band. My ability to play was an expectation, but my team spirit and positive Attitude got me hired for that job—and many jobs since.

BE OPEN AND PLAY FROM THE HEART

Always Play from the Heart

Being open and playing from the heart is a seminal concept within the CRASH! method. One of my favorite sayings is, "Play from the heart, it will set you apart." If your entire focus is on the bottom line, you will not create the kind of culture you want for your team or for yourself. You can tell when someone has their heart in their actions. It makes a difference; people will always notice.

One reason my Attitude remains so consistently

positive is because I invest lots of time and attention into ensuring that my work remains aligned with my true purpose in life. Briefly stated, my purpose in life is to "affect people positively and change lives." Everything I do serves this purpose. If you can identify and serve your life's purpose with your work, then your Attitude cannot help but remain positive.

Have you figured out what your purpose is yet? If not, how do you know if what you are doing is right for you?

ASK YOURSELF TWO FUNDAMENTAL QUESTIONS

- What is the nature of my job?
- Who am I ultimately serving?

If you aren't satisfied with your answers to these questions, then you may need to consider changing jobs to an opportunity more aligned with your purpose.

Even if you are unsatisfied with your current job, working with a positive Attitude will lead to a better opportunity. Your dream job is right around the corner if you infuse your work with enthusiasm and positivity.

My role within Jason Aldean's band has lasted nearly two decades because that band is a vehicle for my purpose. My Attitude shines when I play in that band because I understand my role in that environment. I know what I am supposed to do, and I execute my work every day with a smile on my face. I got that job by excelling in many musical situations and by impressing people who then trusted me enough to recommend me to someone else.

No one will buy your product or service until they have bought into you as a person. Every time you perform in life, you are advertising your product. That product is *you*.

EMBRACE CHANGE

Be open to suggestions. You have to try new things and be willing to change your routine. I may have to audition different beats, a football player may need to run different routes, and an actor may be asked to say lines differently. We are all servants to our work, and must be willing—and happy—to take suggestions.

I have witnessed many situations in the recording studio where a paid musician was difficult to work with. They developed a bad Attitude when forced to adapt to in-the-moment changes during a recording session. When that happens, everyone becomes uncomfortable, and that musician is never called again. Over time, if their Attitude doesn't change, they develop an unfavorable reputation.

In my opinion, a person's reputation is everything. Why jeopardize that?

GOOD VIBES

Intuition is our birthright. All people can sense and feel when someone is thinking negative thoughts. Advances in neuroscience and technology are beginning to measure the fact that negative thought patterns actually manifest themselves on a molecular level. I've certainly been at recording sessions where morale has slipped and the negativity was so thick in the air that you could cut it with a knife.

Fortunately, the reverse is also true. I have eased tensions with a witty joke or by expressing how excited I was to be there and be part of the project.

Let Your Attitude Shine

Experiment with cultivating positivity in this way, even if it seems contrived at first. You'll like the results, not only with other people, but also within yourself. This is a great illustration of how having a positive Attitude can actually improve Relationships.

I work regularly with a rhythm section in Nashville comprised of Kurt Allison, Tully Kennedy, and myself. One night, over too many Irish coffees, we decided to call ourselves "The Three Kings," and the name stuck. We work at the same Nashville studio 90% of the time, and recently the studio manager pulled us aside and told us he loved having us around because there is always a positive energy in the building when we work there. We let our attitudes shine, and as a result, we attract other like-minded people who end up booking their sessions at that studio. That's a great scenario for a studio owner!

PLAYING WITH ATTITUDE

As it relates specifically to drumming, I can't have a conversation about Attitude without discussing all the amazing drummers throughout history that inspired me with their Attitudes. Without hesitation, I think of Gene Krupa (Benny Goodman), John Bonham (Led Zeppelin), Tony Williams (Miles Davis), Carmine Appice (Rod Stewart), Kenny Aronoff (John Mellencamp), Tommy Lee (Motley Crue), Alex Van Halen (Van Halen), Dave Grohl (Nirvana) and many others.

I'm not talking about ego or arrogance here. I'm referring to an utter confidence in their playing and their approach to music that lit a fire of inspiration under all the musicians they played with. More importantly, they could draw the listener into their special world, even if the listener knew nothing about drumming.

World-class athletes like Michael Jordan, Pele, and Wayne Gretzky also come to mind. These gentlemen transformed the sports of basketball, soccer, and ice hockey. Everyone knew they were seeing something special when they saw these guys play. People with a passionate Attitude have charisma. Charismatic individuals get preferential seating at restaurants, win elections, and can even convince a whole country to go to war!

QUALITY CONTROL

I am hired on a regular basis to bring someone else's vision to life. My drums are miked up and recorded into top quality equipment by an engineer or producer regularly. It's my job to bring a positive attitude to my work environment and give it everything I have. Once my performance is recorded and captured onto a piece of tape or a hard drive, I no longer have control. The placements of my beats and musical phrases—even the actual *sound* of my drums—can be altered after the fact by the producer or engineer. Once I leave the recording studio, I'm out of the picture.

Most of us only have control over the individual elements of a larger project or job. With that in mind, we should approach the things we *can* control with positivity, grace, humor, and elbow grease. Let's give hell to the things we can control.

YOUR ATTITUDE ABOUT YOURSELF

THE DEFINITION OF SUCCESS IS THE ABILITY TO WALK FROM FAILURE TO FAILURE WITH NO LOSS OF ENTHUSIASM.

—WINSTON CHURCHILL

There is tremendous power in playing with Attitude. Your Attitude is important not only for other people, but also for yourself. When you carry a fire inside you, everyone notices.

How is your Attitude creating your experiences in life? What does your inner dialogue sound like? Are you encouraging, or self-critical? Do you put yourself down, or build yourself up? What permission do you give yourself to try new things? How do you limit yourself? It's very difficult to achieve greatness with a negative inner dialogue. Be a fan of *you!*

If you're thinking this sounds like a quasi-spiritual exercise, you aren't far off. But it's difficult to frame an intention regarding external behavior without paying attention to internal dynamics. For instance, I know that playing the drums is the way I express myself spiritually and physically. It's the physical manifestation of who I am as a person. Because I've paid attention to attaining this self-realization, I am able to realize my purpose when I play.

Playing with Attitude

My job provides me a platform to share love and light with the world. While on tour, I usually have a dedicated camera operator that shares the stage with me. It's their job to capture passionately performed and eye-catching moments for the video production team. The production team then blasts these images on giant forty-foot screens so the folks in the cheap seats can see and feel the onstage energy. I'm always hamming it up and having a great time with my camera operator. I feel as though we are a team, and our job is to create memorable moments for the audience.

All of the cameramen or -women are given a dedicated person each night that helps roll their cables and makes sure they don't get tangled or trip over them. I'll usually send my over-the-top energy in their direction by smiling at them, high-fiving them, or sharing my onstage drink with them during those hot touring months. These folks are usually blown away that a drummer in a popular band would take the time to do this. I do it because I love people. I want to share my positive attitude and energy with them. I love everyone. I want to meet everyone. It's that simple.

In my experience, as soon as I step near my drum set, I assume a certain Attitude that originates inside of me and flows outward. I own every second of my drumming, from the first click of my sticks to the very last cymbal crash. I am performing before I step on stage and all the way through the final stick toss to a crazed and appreciative fan. I'm always playing with as much Attitude as I can muster. I always maintain that Attitude of passionate confidence while remaining coachable and open to musical and verbal suggestions from my fellow musicians. Is this how you conduct your business? Is this how you play your sport? Is this how you engage with those you care about?

If not, it should be.

CRASH! CHALLENGE QUESTIONS

1. Are you passionate about what you do? Work on doing things that make you happy and stay in that zone as much as possible.
2. How can you cultivate a positive attitude?
3. How can you foster a positive inner dialogue?
4. Are you "playing from the heart" daily? What would it take to make sure you can?
5. How can you add value to other's lives?

CHAPTER 4
SKILL

> WE ARE WHAT WE REPEATEDLY DO.
> EXCELLENCE, THEN, IS NOT AN ACT, BUT A
> HABIT.
>
> —ARISTOTLE

Develop Your Skill

E very day is a new opportunity to sharpen our Skills. Raw talent can be found anywhere, but it's the people who take the time to develop and practice their talents who become real champions in life. We are living in a performance-based world. We are all constantly being evaluated and we have to constantly exceed expectations, no matter the area of our Skills. Whether you're preparing for a job or doing the job, always be on fire.

When I was a young man, I practiced before, during, and after school every day. I wanted to improve and become a great musician. Gigantic thanks to Mom and Dad for putting up with the noise for years. I spent countless hours developing my drumming Skills. There is simply no substitute for many years of practice.

Hard work beats raw talent. Every. Single. Time. I was fortunate to have raw talent, but I focused and developed that by working hard.

Most likely, the expectations and demands of your profession or vocation are increasing every day. To meet these demands and keep up with change and innovation, you must continuously practice relevant Skills and learn new ones.

What are the Skills required for success in your field? What techniques are necessary to achieve the goals you have set for yourself? Have you mastered them? Do you *continue* to practice them?

THE ART OF THE GROOVE

Working together for the greater good is a Skill set. If you are part of a team, it's important to make sure that every member of the team shines in their individual pursuits. You can accomplish that by ignoring your ego and devoting yourself to the good of the group. When you act selflessly, everyone benefits—even you.

For drummers, our role in a band is to keep time while also making things groove. The art of grooving is a Skill learned from studying the great drummers in history and emulating their feel. I have refined this Skill by constantly playing with great musicians who held me accountable to the groove.

Teaching a Master Class

Drummers need to have a certain level of four-limb coordination that allows us to play with a fusion of precision and feeling. This fusion is what separates the good from the truly excellent in every area of life. This is multitasking at its highest level. If you want advice on multitasking, talk to a drummer.

Grooving is a magical place where every facet of your job comes together in perfect harmony. Everything feels right: you are creative, focused, productive, and happy. Another term for this is being in the zone. You can tell when you're in the zone not only by the way it makes you feel, but by the way you are affecting others.

When you're grooving, you inspire others to join you in that place. The goal is to be in the groove as often as we can.

> - How do you know if you are helping things groove in your world?
> - How do you continue to learn from the greats in your profession, past and present, to steadily deliver in your role?

A salesperson, speaker, or preacher, is grooving when they're coordinating eye contact, voice tone, body language, and message. A writer is grooving when the words feel like they're pouring out and there's no need to reference the outline or question a phrase. A teacher is grooving when the students are engaged with the lesson, asking the right questions, and participating in the discussion. Whatever it is you do, can you tell if you are grooving? I bet you can!

THE THREE PS

> When it comes to success, remember the three Ps:
>
> - PEOPLE SKILLS
> - PERSISTENCE
> - PRESENCE

PEOPLE SKILLS

People Skills can be just as important as your job Skills—if not more important. If you want to improve your people Skills, consider the golden rule. Ask yourself: how would I like to be treated? If you the answer is: with respect and compassion, then you must treat others the same way.

One way to do that is to focus on perfecting your bedside manner. If I am presented with a doctor that takes time to evaluate me as a whole person, or one that spends two minutes not looking me in the eye and quickly writing a prescription, I will choose the doctor who has both the medical Skills *and* the ability to view me as a human being worthy of respect.

Which doctor would you prefer to see? Which doctor would you prefer to *be?*

PERSISTENCE

> ENERGY AND PERSISTENCE CONQUER ALL THINGS.
>
> —BENJAMIN FRANKLIN

Polite persistence will get you everywhere in life. Success does not happen overnight, and you have to stay Committed. Anything worth doing is going to be full of challenges and obstacles. Be unwavering in your focus and let nothing stop you, but don't hurt people or burn bridges. Keep fostering positive Relationships, building your Skills, and maintaining a pleasant Attitude in all of your interactions.

With Sarra Cardile at My Third Annual
Drummer's Weekend Nashville, 2015

I have had many students over the years, but one in particular who exemplifies CRASH! is Sarra Cardile. Sarra is Hungry for success, and she is actively creating opportunities using polite persistence through social media and interactions with drummers at local music venues. Her ability to use people skills to foster deeper relationships are paying off. She played a soundcheck with my band and everyone enjoyed the experience. She was invited up on stage to play with recording artists Big and Rich. Sarra lives the CRASH! concept, and with the support of her family, is well on her way to success.

PRESENCE

In a society of distraction and constant connection to social media updates and notifications, give people in your life the gift of your presence. In other words, your undivided attention. I purposely place my cell phone face down on the table when I am having a meeting with someone.

Try this technique the next time you're in a social situation or a business meeting. Keeping the phone notifications off and putting the phone face down lets you stay focused without distractions. Follow that up with eye contact and truly be committed to staying present in that moment. Life is a collection of experiences, and it's important to make those experiences positive for everyone around you.

If you have a team player mentality, people will line up to work with you. In my field, that means taking direction from bandleaders, recording artists, and producers. I never take suggestions or criticisms personally. I try to have a positive servant Attitude and to give, give, give. Taking direction and criticism without being offended or becoming angry is a Skill that will make people remember you and recommend you to their friends. Ask yourself this question: am I easy to work with? If there is a hesitation before your answer, then consider what you can do to be a better collaborator.

Remember: a highly developed Skill set steeped in positivity and enthusiasm is always a winning combination.

TEN THOUSAND HOURS OF PRACTICE

In the famous book *Outliers*, author Malcolm Gladwell claimed that it takes roughly ten thousand hours of practicing to master a Skill. Gladwell offered examples ranging from Bill Gates to the Beatles to support his hypothesis. Many academics criticized Gladwell's claim and showed that, although Commitment to practice is important, simply logging ten thousand hours won't turn you into a master of your craft. But that doesn't mean practice isn't important.

Demonstrating the Results of Ten Thousand Hours

Repetitive practice does play a role in the development of any Skill, whether physical, interpersonal, or intellectual. The more you repeat something, the more embedded in your muscles and neural pathways it becomes. This is what is known as muscle memory, or the mind-body connection. You may not have been born with the Skill, but you've practiced it so much it seems totally natural to any observer.

When I was practicing for my college classical percussion recitals, I would drill individual musical phrases for hours at a time. I would 'burn' the exercise into my subconscious and muscles with pure repetition.

On every tour I have done with Aldean, some life event has happened to the drummers in the opening act—Luke Bryan, Thomas Rhett, Thompson Square, Halfway to Hazard, etc. I have filled in for the drummers, sometimes for a planned event, and sometimes in an emergency. The only reason I was able to do that was because of my deep Skill set, which allowed me to step into the role of the drummer. If I had enough notice, I would do sound checks and shows for both acts, including a costume change, which requires a lot of energy and focus. It was a fun challenge, but it allowed me to fulfill my purpose of helping other people.

Reading Music is a Skill that Has Helped Me Many Times

If I hadn't had my Skills—ten thousand hours of practice, the ability to read music, my ability to blend with others as a team player and take direction well under pressure—I wouldn't have been able to help make sure the show could go on for our fans and audience. Everyone wants to save the day. Don't you?

My advice is to identify the Skills you'll need to be successful in your chosen field and *master* them. Whatever Skills you require, practice them until they become second nature, and also always try to learn *new* Skills, pushing yourself beyond your current comfort zone.

CRASH! CHALLENGE QUESTIONS

1. What are the Skills you need to be successful in your field? Write them down.
2. How do you know when you are grooving?
3. Do you consistently treat others the way you wish to be treated? If not, start.
4. Can you take suggestions without being offended? If not, why?
5. What new Skills are you working on developing?

CHAPTER 5

HUNGER

Hungry to Give Audiences the Best Show of Their Lives

O f all the elements of CRASH!, Hunger is not about something you have or develop. Hunger is about something you *don't* have. It is a need unmet, a desire not satisfied, a void unfulfilled. You should always have a Hunger that burns inside—one that connects you firmly to your dreams and goals and helps you share those dreams with the world.

Even after you've achieved your goals, you have to stay

Hungry. You can never think you have earned the right to stop developing and growing. You have to kill complacency because complacency kills. Hunger is a driving force that propels you to take massive action, and that's a good thing.

A FIRE AND AN EMPTINESS

The Best Seat in the House

When it comes to the CRASH! formula, Hunger is both a driving force or fuel, and an unmet need. It's not just a fire, but also an emptiness, which drives a desire for more than what you have now. Hunger is crucial, not only for igniting the other CRASH! elements, but for fueling them along your journey. It is undoubtedly the most primal one: the first state that exists before you invest the time and energy into making Commitments, building Relationships, fostering Attitudes, and developing Skills.

When I first arrived in Nashville, my Hunger for drumming success resulted in credit cards maxed out from purchasing ramen noodles and Balance Bars. Both physically and psychologically this was a leaner time, but it was a special time. Every day, I would feverishly and enthusiastically work to make my dreams a reality. I had a burning Hunger for success. I was starving to perform on the world's stage. I wanted to play on records, hear myself on the radio, and travel the world on someone else's dime. I had a burning desire to be part of the crazy culture that was the music business.

Playing with Fire . . . Literally

In 1997, my bags were packed for sunny Los Angeles when I received a call to audition for a major-label recording artist in Nashville. Two more auditions for major label artists followed. Airline tickets, rental cars, and hotel expenses all went on my ever-expanding credit card bill. I was willing to do whatever it took to take my career to the next level. Bills could always be paid, but it was my time to make my dreams happen. I was Hungry.

You know that feeling you get in your stomach when you realize you have been working hard all day long and haven't eaten? That was the feeling I had burning in my heart. I wanted it, but more than that, I needed it.

There is a difference between "want to" and "have to." Can you remember what made you want to do what you do? Tap into those feelings and let that drive you.

Once a week or even once a day, ask yourself what you really want. I don't just want to play the drums, I *need* to. It's what defines me, and more importantly, what makes me happy.

Let passion be your engine and hard work be your fuel. When you are passionate about something, it makes it easy to work hard. The harder you work, the more opportunities and success come to you.

A Dream That Would Eventually Come True:
Playing Iconic Stadiums Like Fenway Park

STARVING ARTISTS

When I moved to Nashville I was operating on pure desire, blind faith in myself, and a burning Hunger to taste success. I was playing clubs, pick up gigs, honky-tonks, weddings, free demo sessions, and showcases, but I was now doing those things in a place where there were endless possibilities for career advancement. In Nashville, I could get that Big Gig.

I waited tables, substitute taught, worked construction, and took every gig that came across my path. It was a very exciting time in my life. When you are in the battle to bring your life's dreams to fruition, it is a time of endless possibilities, frustrating setbacks, and tantalizing victories. I've learned it's impossible to succeed at anything without failing many times. Learn from your setbacks and use them to fuel future successes . . . and don't forget to celebrate every little victory!

When I moved to Nashville, people were still using pagers (I know—what's a pager, right?). I used to pull off the side of the road in search of pay phones to return pages from potential employers. It was like Christmas morning every time that thing started buzzing. Most of the time it was just my mother calling to check on me (ha!). For a long time when I called back the professional contacts, the conversations went something like this: "Hey Rich. I got your number from John Smith. Are you available to play from 10 pm–2:30 am on Monday night for forty dollars and free beer?" Before the voice on the other end could finish talking, my answer was always "YES!"

In those days, I also had an answering machine

connected to the landline in my apartment. One day, I got a message like this: "Rich, Paul gave me your number and said you might be available to play in Korea and Japan for a month. Back line gear, comfortable travel, accommodations, meals provided, and tons of great sightseeing. Interested?" I said, "Yes" to that one before I even found out what it paid! Thankfully, it ended up also being a good paying job. My patience and persistence, fueled by my Hunger, had begun to pay off.

I stayed in the game, and the calls (and pages) continued to become more fruitful. I paid my dues, and that paid dividends. I can even remember playing pickup gigs until 3 a.m., getting home by 4, getting two hours of sleep, and being in front of a classroom full of kindergartners as a substitute teacher at 7 a.m.

That's Commitment. That's Hunger.

STAY HUNGRY

Today, I still make it a point to study the habits of successful people, and what I've noticed is that at a certain point, things can become comfortable. People start taking things for granted, they get complacent, they lose their spark, and the quality of their work starts to decline.

Don't let this happen to you!

Individuals and organizations who consistently reinvent themselves, develop new Skill sets, and create new product lines are the ones who survive and continue to thrive. People greatly respect individuals or companies that never rest on past accomplishments. When you fan the flames of Hunger and keep pushing, you will be rewarded with new and exciting opportunities. In other words, you get back what you put in. The lesson: Stay Hungry!

Hungry to Teach and to Share Knowledge and Experience

PINCH ME!

There are nights in my life that I just can't believe. Imagine this: someone has set up a set of drums for me. A road manager shouts, "Five minutes." I then get onto a golf cart with a police escort that takes me to a stage set up in a football stadium. 80,000 screaming fans await. I take the stage to a deafening roar of the crowd. I sweat my brains out and give the band and the audience everything I have for ninety minutes. I toss my sticks into the hands of an appreciative fan, get back on the golf cart and cruise to a tour bus. Dripping with sweat, I get on the tour bus that leaves the city with a police escort.

What? Is this my life? How did this happen? Oh yeah ... hard work. It happened, I celebrate daily . . .

but . . . now what? What's next? I'm still so hungry for new levels of life adventures.

Musicians, athletes, and business leaders who I respect and model myself after are the ones that sound and look like they are literally playing for their supper. No matter what stage of their career they are in, they are Hungry. They want it. The only way for them to feed their Hunger is to always perform at the top of their game. They play like it's the last time they will ever pick up their instrument, take the field, or launch a new product.

Fast-forward many years from that day I arrived in Nashville. Countless recording studios, rehearsal halls, tour buses, hotels, and backstage areas have come and gone. They could easily all run together, but they don't. I'm making sure that I drink it in, express and truly feel gratitude, and stay Hungry.

To me, the word HUNGER conjures up positive images of someone passionately, purposefully, and relentlessly pursuing a dream. What is your dream, and are you willing to go Hungry for it? These are important questions to ask— and even more important ones to answer.

Still Hungry for More Success

What you are Hungry *for* may change over time. That might become a concern, or it might be an invitation to reframe your Commitment to yourself. For myself, I have achieved my initial goals, and I am now Hungry for new worlds to conquer.

And it's because of CRASH! that I'll make those dreams come true as well.

CRASH! CHALLENGE QUESTIONS

1. What makes you happy and fulfilled? Write it down.
2. What do you want most out of life? Write it down.
3. Do you just *want* to do it, or do you *have* to do it? Why? Write it down.
4. What are you willing to do to get it? Write it down.
5. How will you stay Hungry?

CHAPTER 6
A KID FROM CONNECTICUT

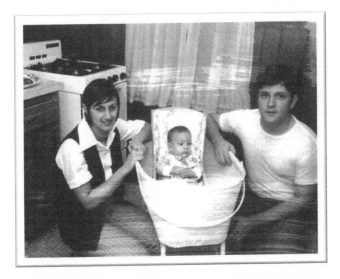

With My Parents, Patricia and Richard Redmond

was using the CRASH! formula long before I became
consciously aware of what I was doing or how I was doing
it. But now, looking back over my life, I can see how the
interplay of Commitment, Relationships, Attitude, Skill,
and Hunger helped me realize my dream.

The reason for sharing some of my personal journey with you is because, if I was able to *unconsciously* utilize the elements of CRASH! for success in my own story, how much more powerful might they be for you if you got to use them *intentionally?*

A TYPICAL FAMILY

My Parents' Wedding   *Baby Rich*

I'm just a kid from Connecticut living what I call the "Unicorn Dream"—you know, the one that seems impossible until it actually happens. I was born on July 25, 1970, in Norwich, Connecticut. My mother, Patricia Francis Paradiso, was also born in Connecticut and is of Italian descent. My father, Richard Dale Redmond, was born in Delaware, and served in the US Navy on submarines. Dad became an accountant in his civilian career, while Mom became a nurse, and both of my parents have only recently retired.

I have two younger brothers named Jason and Michael. I'm six years older than Jason and nine years older than Michael. All three of us have carved out very different career paths. Jason has a big family and loves to fish and hunt. Mike is single and is very private.

With My Brothers, Jason and Michael

I'm definitely the black sheep of the family. I'm the only person in my family to ever be a professional musician. I was always a type A, restless kid with a lot of energy. That's a word that has been a theme in my life. People always say to me: "Rich, I wish I had your energy," even if they're half my age or younger! I've inherited both of my parents' perspectives and energy styles, which has really helped me in life.

A HIGH-ENERGY PERSONALITY

One of the laws of physics is that energy cannot be created

or destroyed, but only transferred, and I think I inherited my visible kinetic energy from my mother. My mom beat breast cancer in 1986 and ran a marathon a year later. To say she's an inspiring person is an understatement. She's very energetic, and although she's "retired" now, she's busier than she's ever been. Now that she's had her career as a nurse and raised a family, she has continued to focus her energy on things that give her personal fulfillment. I can't envision myself as totally retiring, either. This is one reason why I'm exploring other opportunities to remain creatively and personally fulfilled for the rest of my life.

Milford, Connecticut

My father has an amazing work ethic that I'm glad to have inherited. When we lived in Connecticut, my dad worked at a bakery and went to night school for six years to become an accountant. His Commitment to his career helped form my Attitude toward work at a young age. I always had a paper route and I shoveled snow and raked leaves for money. As a good accountant, Dad looked at the risk side of every equation. He would outline the risks of my career decisions, but he always supported my choices. Who could ask for more than that?

With My Parents at My Aunt Pam's Wedding

I think deep down my dad loved the drums, and he intuitively understood that drumming would give me a channel for all my energy. One day when I was six years old, he asked me if I wanted to take drum lessons and I said, "Yes!"

I took my first drum lessons at the Milford Percussion and Guitar Workshop. My first teacher there was a man named Jack Berkey. Jack told my parents that I had tons of natural ability and was far beyond other players my age. Even though everyone was happy that I could drum so well at such a young age, I was also just a kid with a banana bike and a skateboard, and I still wanted to play with my *Star Wars* figures. So, I took a break.

Little did I know that I had found my calling; I was just too young to appreciate what I had discovered.

My First Drum Set, 1977

CHAPTER 7
THE KID FROM EL PASO

Band Class, 1981

n 1981, I was eleven years old. My dad got a big promotion, and we moved to El Paso, Texas. Dad was now the manager of a *Maquiladora* (border factory). We lived in the US, and he crossed the border into Mexico every day for work.

I was in fifth grade. My brother Jason was five, and my brother Michael was two. I was looking to fit in at my new school, so I joined the Fifth Grade Band. I had taken a short break from drumming from age seven to eleven, but because of those early lessons in Connecticut, my Skills were more developed than those of the other kids'.

The move to Texas worked out well for me because Texas has always had great music education programs. At the time, drumming was just something I knew how to do—something to help me fit in as the new kid. This was the first time in my life that I realized being good at something could help me gain respect and have a positive impact on other people's perceptions of me.

I felt happy because I was doing something that I now really liked. I enjoyed the social affirmation and acceptance I received from being a good drummer.

Fifth Grade Band

THE CATALYST YEARS

I started school in Texas at Pebble Hill Elementary School. Then I went to Desert View Middle School for seventh and eighth grade. From the CRASH! perspective, my Commitment to being a drummer started in the middle school years. Those two years are my "catalyst years." That was the time when I knew drumming was what I was going to do with my life. I was lucky to have found my passion and my purpose at thirteen years old.

1983 was the Golden Age of the music video. MTV broadcast music videos together with live concerts around the clock, and the VJ's themselves—Martha Quinn, JJ Jackson, Alan Hunter, and Nina Blackwood—were very dynamic people. While I was studying the drummers in the videos, I confess I had a huge crush on Martha Quinn.

In June 1983, The Police released an album called *Synchronicity* that was all the rage. You could say this record was my gateway drug to a career in music. Stewart Copeland, the drummer from The Police, was a big influence on my drumming. The next year, Van Halen released their album *1984*, and I fell in love with the drumming of Alex Van Halen.

At the same time, my Dad bought me my first professional-quality drum set. It was a cherry red Yamaha stage custom kit, which had 13", 14", 18", and 24" drums. Those drums were huge and magnificent! I used to polish those things every time I played; I was so proud of them. And I didn't just play a few times a week, or even once a day. I would practice before school, during my music classes, at lunch, and after school, every day. When my other friends went out to lunch, I brown-bagged it with a peanut butter and jelly sandwich so I could practice my drums.

From seventh grade all the way through high school, my Hunger grew and grew, and fed my Commitment to excellence. I was very serious in terms of my inner goal: "I'm going to be the best at this school, and the best in the state!" My plan wasn't crystallized. I had stars in my eyes, but I didn't know how to achieve my dreams except to practice, practice, practice. I believed that if I just kept practicing, the path to musical success would be revealed.

OUT-PASSIONING MY RIVALS

J.M. Hanks High School

After finishing middle school in 1984, I attended J.M. Hanks High School. By this time, I was fully immersed in my drumming passion and so I joined every music ensemble the school had to offer: concert band, marching band, orchestra, jazz band, everything.

On the first day of high school, I met drumline captain

Richard, a cocky junior who played in all the best groups. I knew that if I wanted to get to his position, I'd have to be better than him.

So, I got to work. I worked so hard that I "out-passioned" him and out-focused him, and he ended up losing interest in music and changing direction for the rest of his high school career. Competition is a fact of life in every vocation. I believe healthy competition is an extremely useful tool, which can help drive us to become better.

Ultimately, I became the drumline captain, the jazz band drum set player, and the section leader of the concert band percussion section. And for the next three years, our school's music groups did really well and won many awards. This fueled my confidence and conviction to devote my life to making music.

While in high school, I had a music teacher named Henry Vega. I knew that I wanted to be the first-chair percussion of the Texas All-State Concert Band. Texas is a huge state, and the music program was just as big. I would need to beat out roughly eight thousand other high school drummers to achieve my dream.

Although some people might have found these daunting odds, my strong Commitment to developing my Skills was already lending me a lot of confidence.

Mr. Vega rehearsed with me before school, at lunch, and after school to help me with my dream. For my part, I worked really hard, and I ended up winning that position two years in a row.

My love for the drums was aligned with my purpose, and I knew that if I worked hard enough, I could achieve anything. I've been putting this formula to work ever since.

On the Drumline with Coke-Bottle Glasses

MARCHING TO MY OWN BEAT

I was a straight-A student in high school. I had coke-bottle glasses at the time and loved to play Dungeons and Dragons. There, I said it, and I did take some ribbing from the jocks and cool kids at the school. I walked fast, talked fast, I wore high-waters, and I was a little cocky. But looking back now, it seems like even the people who hassled me had a kind of grudging respect. It felt as if something deep down in them was saying, "This kid is *focused*, this kid works hard, and when he plays the drums . . . he's good! He's got something."

So yes, I was the guy in the talent show with the heavy metal band wearing coke-bottle glasses. People would say, "he might not *look* cool, but he *plays* cool."

Negative people couldn't sway me from my purpose, though. I was too busy and focused. If the cool kids hassled me, I'd just keep walking right past them—I was probably on my way to practice.

REAL LIFE MENTORS

I've always been lucky to have great teachers who believed in me. I took lessons from a teacher named Byron Mutnick. He had hundreds of students, but he would say things to my parents like, "You know, I have to stay one step ahead of your son, because he's the only one of my students who comes in prepared." Even during this early chapter of my life, I knew that preparation was the key to being good at anything.

Another teacher I recall, who was part-owner of the local music store, was named Jamie Olivas. Mr. Olivas was an accomplished jazz saxophone player and my high school jazz band director at JM Hanks High School. My school was so underfunded that we didn't have a drum set, so my dad had to cart drums around in the back of his Toyota pickup.

One day after Dad dropped off my drums, Mr. Olivas took the time to pull him aside and say, "Your son's going to do well in the music business because he has a great Attitude and can take direction without being offended. This will serve him well." This really stuck with me. The ability to be coachable and accept criticism is key to a successful life.

The affirmation and encouragement I received from teachers like Mr. Mutnick and Mr. Olivas had a profound impact on me and helped reassure my parents that I was on the right track. This is why today, despite everything you can learn online, I encourage people to have a real-life teacher.

Having that personal Relationship will keep you

supported, motivated, and accountable. Whatever Skill set you seek to improve, I firmly believe that an in-person Relationship with a trusted teacher or mentor is invaluable.

High School Drumline (I'm on the Far Right, in Sunglasses)

THE DRUM SET AS MY MISTRESS

Because of my Commitment to drumming, when it came to girls, I didn't have a lot of time. I was well-adjusted and I always had a girlfriend, but my Relationships paled in comparison to my Commitment to my craft.

I would try to snatch five minutes with a girl, maybe grab a sandwich together, and then I'd say, "Okay! See you later! Gotta go!" And I'd go back to playing the drums. At that time, and possibly always, the drum set was my mistress.

My High School Talent Show, 1985

COMMITMENT TO TECHNIQUE

As I was refining my Skills as a young musician, I developed my own system for practice. If I was having problems with one section of a piece of music, I would use the challenging section as an exercise and focus on it very methodically. I would practice that section every day until I could perform it perfectly ten times in a row. I used this technique for percussion recitals in college and on every major audition I've ever had, to this day.

Little did I know that during my time in El Paso I was developing the elements that would one day become CRASH! I was very Committed to my craft, and I had a great Attitude that helped me build Relationships with teachers. I was very focused on becoming the best at what I did, and I practiced like mad. My Hunger burned brightly as I worked on my Skills daily. I had a laser focus.

NEED TO CONNECT

Many people have a desire to excel, but don't have a plan. My advice to them is to use this advice from the great Dr. Martin Luther King, Jr.: "Take the first step in faith. You don't have to see the whole staircase, just take the first step." I had already taken those first steps, and I was committed to developing my Skills. I was also taking lessons from the best teachers in the city: people like Ricky Malachi, Larry White, Jim Hargrove, and Byron Mutnik. I knew I would wind up on the big stage, but I didn't know how I was going to get there.

El Paso, the farthest point in secluded west Texas, is a wonderful city steeped in rich cultural traditions, but unfortunately none of those were connected to the music business. I'd been voraciously reading *Modern Drummer* magazine as early as 1983, and all the guys I would read about in those pages lived in New York City or Los Angeles. It seemed apparent to me that I would have to go to one of those places.

But first, college. My dad and I agreed that I would study music at the university level, and I knew that was something that would help me increase my Skill set. The only questions were: where, and with whom?

CHAPTER 8

RELATIONSHIPS AND RED
RAIDERS

EVERY GREAT ACHIEVEMENT IS THE STORY OF
A FLAMING HEART.

-RALPH WALDO EMERSON

The Texas Tech Drumline, 1988

I considered two schools for college: The University of
North Texas and Texas Tech University. I visited Texas
Tech the summer before my senior year in high school,
and I met Professor Alan Shinn, who was the head of the

percussion department at the time. After listening to me play, Alan talked to my dad and said, "I will get your son a scholarship and he will play every day."

So, I went to Texas Tech, and Alan was true to his word; I played all day, every day: percussion ensemble, marching band, symphonic band, new music ensemble, small-group jazz ensemble, big-group jazz ensemble—that's a lot of playing! I used those four years of college to offset the reality of the real world while increasing my Skill level in a safe environment.

By this time, I was firing on all but one cylinder of the CRASH! model, even though I didn't yet know it. The Commitment was there, the Hunger was there, and my Skills were developing at a feverish pace. I always had a good Attitude as well; I always knew to be positive. I never burned a bridge, and I strove to surround myself with as many like-minded people as I could. The only things I was missing were the Relationships in the industry that could catapult my career forward.

IN LOVE WITH THE DRUMS

Abraham Lincoln once said, "Whatever you are, be a good one." I agree, but I would take it even further: whatever you are, be a *great* one. I had a burning desire to become a professional drummer, and that Hunger fed an intrinsic need to be excellent.

I was so focused on being the best drummer that I could become obsessed. I'm sure my brothers thought I was crazy, and they weren't the only ones. I remember we would have big family gatherings at the holidays, and people would ask,

"Where's Richie?"

I would be in my parents' closet, practicing. I hung blankets over the doors, hoping the clothes would absorb the sound without disturbing my neighbors and relatives too much.

Most truly successful people are obsessed with their field. I told myself that if I wanted to go to Los Angeles and break into the profession, I would have to become as good as the drummers out there. Nobody was going to do the work for me.

I didn't know anyone in Los Angeles. When you don't have Relationships, Skill becomes even more important. I would need to be ridiculously proficient across a number of styles for people to take notice.

TEACHING IS A GREAT TEACHER

> IN LEARNING YOU WILL TEACH, AND IN TEACHING YOU WILL LEARN.
>
> -PHIL COLLINS

There are few things that can reinforce a Skill set better than teaching those Skills to others. I started teaching drum lessons in the summer between freshman and sophomore year at Texas Tech when I was nineteen years old.

That summer, I got my first real job in a working Tejano band called *Pueblo*. We played in nightclubs all over El Paso. For the first time, I was making money as a working drummer. I was so excited, and I came in playing with a bit more flourish than the music required. There was this very experienced conga player who told me in no uncertain terms, "You play time, I solo!"

This gentleman put me in my place. Although he was impressed with my child-like enthusiasm for drumming, he needed me to play basic beats. This was humbling. It helped me get into the mindset of being an accompanist. This was when I truly realized that I was no longer there for myself, but I was part of a team. My job was not to showcase my Skills, but to make the other musicians sound great.

This was the first time that the hours spent practicing in a dark room by myself were finally being utilized in front of a paid audience. I grew so much that summer that when I went back to college for my second year, the teachers noticed my improvement. After years in strictly academic institutions, I finally had some street cred, and it felt great.

AN UNIDENTIFIED HUNGER

But even though I had a taste of working as a musician, I still had no idea how the music business really worked.

This is the problem with a lot of music education—and many educational programs in general. They teach basic Skills, but not what to do with those Skills once you're out of the program. There is no discussion, education, or mentoring about the realities of business. The focus at a school like Texas Tech University is more classical pedagogy: "I will teach you to play well, but not how to find work playing." This is true outside of academia as well. Skills training does not always prepare employees for what they will truly need to know in order to succeed in real-life situations.

We're doing students a disservice by showing them all the various parts of the fish and fishing rod, but not actually teaching them how to cast and catch a fish. Existing educational programs should be meshed with the practical ideology of vocational programs, especially in the creative fields where many students don't have a natural business acumen.

Now, I see it as a duty to go back to music programs such as my alma mater and help students bridge the gap between academia and the real world of the music industry.

NURTURING EARLY RELATIONSHIPS

No matter how Skilled I was, if people didn't know about me, I would never get my shot. Developing my professional network was the next crucial stage in my development, so I became very intentional about building and nurturing Relationships.

There weren't many opportunities for professional Relationships in sleepy Lubbock, Texas, but I did my best with the opportunities that did come along. For instance, when guest artists would visit the school and I got the chance to back them up, I would spend as much time as I could with them, asking a lot of questions and finding out what weaknesses I could improve. I backed up artists like Bob Mintzer, Steve Weist, Billy Hulting, and many other prominent jazz musicians. The feedback I received from them or through my teachers really affirmed my belief that I had the spark—that elusive It factor—to go farther.

I believe part of the reason the guest artists praised me was because when I backed them up, I would play with every ounce of passion and precision I could muster. I brought my A-game every time. Whatever it is you do, remember the CRASH! concepts. Are you working with a level of Commitment and energy that others can't avoid noticing?

I knew it was important to build relationships, so when these famous artists would ask for something, I would quickly oblige. I wanted to impress them with my team spirit and Commitment to a positive Attitude. I went into "servant mode," hoping to form lifelong connections that could potentially pay out in the future. I recognized these people as gatekeepers and I needed to be remembered. Leave your mark wherever you can, as often as you can.

Meanwhile, my ongoing Commitment to my Skill development remained very strong. I recorded all of my concerts and recitals and played them back to hear how I could improve. Doing this is a great learning opportunity. There are few things more helpful than being able to observe your work from an outsider's perspective. Actors, athletes, TV hosts, and radio DJs also listen to or view their work to note any imperfections they can avoid in the future.

- In your field, how do you review your own performance to try to become better?
- If you don't have a system for doing this, how could you create one?

COMPLACENCY IS THE ENEMY

SOMETIMES SUCCESS NEEDS INTERRUPTION TO
REGAIN FOCUS AND SHAKE OFF COMPLACENCY.
-LENNOX LEWIS

I did great things at Texas Tech, but I became a big fish in a small pond, and I ran the risk of becoming complacent. Many people and organizations struggle against complacency when they get to the top of their field. I was nowhere near the top of the drumming world, or even the top in Texas. But I had "arrived" at Texas Tech, and I wasn't being pushed hard enough. I had to rely on my own self-starter mentality.

The students surrounding me weren't following my path. Many of them wanted to be music educators, not full-time, top-call performers, and so there weren't as many people challenging me in my junior and senior years. My teachers noticed that something was off, but because I loved percussion and I was still Hungry for Success, I chose to challenge myself by putting together two ninety-minute recitals mixing a range of drumming styles. These recitals were not a requirement for my degree program, but I did them anyway because I wanted to shine.

When I graduated from Texas Tech, I moved into a world full of challenges at the much more competitive music program at the University of North Texas.

CHAPTER 9
DRUMMING IN DENTON

I'M NEVER SURE ONE IS EXACTLY READY. YOU
JUMP IN, WITH BOTH FEET, INTO A VERY BIG
FISH POND.

- JULIE ANDREWS

I studied with Alan Shinn at Texas Tech from 1988 to 1993. The summer after graduation, my girlfriend Mary and I got married and immediately moved to Dallas, Texas. There, I started the Master's in Education program at the University of North Texas.

The University of North Texas has a world-renowned program with an incredible percussion and jazz department. When I arrived, I was suddenly surrounded by musicians with a laser focus. This school was a truer reflection of what the real world in the music industry would be like: a highly competitive environment. At first it was a little scary to go from the big fish in a small pond to a small fish in a big pond, but being surrounded by those incredibly driven, equally like-minded individuals helped me reframe my goals. I told myself, "I am going to be one of the best drummers here."

IT'S EASY TO BE THE BIG FISH

Anyone who makes it to the next level of their career experiences higher expectations. With those expectations comes the realization that the surrounding people are also playing at a higher level.

As you have progressed in your chosen field, how have you reframed your goals to adjust to higher expectations and more intense competition? Do you continue to do this? If not, how are you avoiding complacency or stagnation?

I quickly began progressing at UNT, and in my first semester I played drums in the Five O'Clock Lab Band and percussion in the Two O'Clock Lab Band. There are twelve lab bands numbered according to Skill, with the One O'Clock Lab Band being the best.

This was a better reflection of the actual music business, especially given that competition for these spots came from all degree levels: Bachelor's, Master's, and Doctorate, meaning that there were 150 drummers competing for those twelve drum chairs. Competing as a twenty-two-year-old against some amazingly talented eighteen-year-old freshmen was a quick cure for complacency.

By the end of my second semester, I had progressed to the point where I was the drum chair for the 1 o'clock lab band, one of the most highly respected collegiate jazz bands on the planet.

To be selected for a position with the band, performers needed the ability to read music. Because I was very good at reading, my Commitment to Skills and willingness to over-prepare got me that first chair.

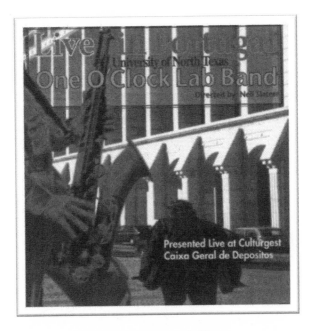

The Live in Portugal *Album*

In 1994, the 1 o'clock lab band recorded a live album in Portugal called *Live in Portugal '94.* I felt tremendous pressure, because everyone who had ever graduated from that band had gone on to have great careers, including drummers like Greg Bissonnette (David Lee Roth/Ringo's All-Star Band), Steve Houghton (jazz great), Ray Brinker (Pat Benatar), and many others. It was a really big honor to be in that kind of company. In the hallways of school, you could hear whispers of, "Who is this guy who just came out of nowhere?"

THE BACKUP PLAN

I never wanted to be a full-time educator, but I'm glad I completed the training for a backup plan. My master's degree has given me an edge even recently. Every college teaching position I have held required a Master's Degree. It has opened doors that would have been closed, and it has taught me Skills I would never have otherwise learned.

Being overqualified and over-prepared has always been a successful business model for me, and it's an easy model for anyone to replicate.

DON'T OVERCOMMIT

> BUT THIS IS LIFE ON EARTH. YOU CAN'T HAVE EVERYTHING.
>
> —WILLIAM GOLDMAN

While I was at North Texas University, I was in school all day and playing five to six nights a week. Because of this, other things in my life were not getting the same level of attention, and my marriage was one of them. Mary worked full time in the hospitality business while I went to school. I was living two lives, practicing relentlessly to compete in the school's academic environment and doing my best to climb the ranks of professional drummers in the Dallas music scene. Mary kept a rigid schedule for her new job and we never saw each other. We passed each other like ships in the night. Trying to learn how to be a good husband had to compete with academic and scheduling pressures, and unfortunately my marriage took the hit.

Neither of us had the insight for how to make a marriage work. What I was Hungry for, and Committed to, wasn't congruent with the Attitude and Commitment necessary for a marriage. Ultimately, a very important Relationship came to an end.

This was my first big aha! moment regarding the management of multiple Commitments. You need to be careful about how many things you commit to at one time. It takes a certain level of maturity and life experience in order to decide how many Commitments you can undertake. Neither Mary nor I were mature enough to make those decisions. The lesson here: don't overcommit.

ACHIEVING BALANCE

It's impossible to have everything. You just can't. If you take too much on and spread yourself too thin, something suffers. This is where the criteria you use to measure success becomes very relevant. If you want to become the best in the world at something, and your life partner is unable to support you for whatever reason, then something somewhere has to give.

There is absolutely nothing wrong with deciding that some early dreams may go unrealized to make room for other Commitments that come along later, or discovering that something you committed to later doesn't fit with your overall life goal.

But the truth is, everything ends. You can't hold on to regret, because you never really know what might have

103

been. If Mary and I had stayed married, I might never have moved to Nashville. If I hadn't moved to Nashville, I wouldn't have been able to lend a hand in changing the sound of modern country music! Through all my trials and tribulations, I remained hyper-focused on my goals and Committed to my journey.

CHAPTER 10
BIG D, LITTLE D, AND THE
DALLAS/FORT WORTH SCENE

THERE ARE NO SHORTCUTS TO ANY PLACE
WORTH GOING.

-BEVERLY SILLS

A Mid-90s Press Shot with Lots of Hair

For the two years after graduation, I kicked around Dallas, playing with anyone and everyone: society bands, smooth jazz bands, big bands, and top-40 bands. I taught lessons, I played on jingles, and played and played and played. I was in a steel drum band, I kicked jokes for comedians, and said "yes" to any gig offered to me.

In school and on the pro scene, I was applying my knowledge with musicians who were better and more experienced than me. This led to a period of tremendous growth. After graduation, I moved to a suburb of Dallas called Farmer's Branch. This was very close to an area of town called Addison. Addison, Texas is an adult playground with restaurants, nightclubs, and bars that feature live music every night of the week. I worked and worked, played and played.

Ultimately, I was faced with the decision to stay on my current path or make a change. These are the same questions that everybody with a goal will ask themselves at some point, whether they are performers, athletes, or business owners.

- How do I take my game to the next level?
- Can I do that here, or do I have to move?

For me, that decision was easy. I had to get out of Dallas! Most of my friends that had graduated with me were heading to the coasts. I knew I had to go to New York or LA. Nashville wasn't even on the radar at that time.

I honored the music and opportunities that I was getting with a great Attitude, my Commitment was still very strong, my Skill set was continuing to develop, and my Hunger was now evolving into wanting something more than what the Dallas music scene had too offer.

I started drumming in Connecticut, then El Paso, then Lubbock, Denton, and then Dallas. With each move, I had to reinvent myself and make new connections. I would have to do that *again* in order to succeed.

I was always very proactive about networking. Getting out and getting noticed was my top priority. If I wasn't booked on a gig, I would go see live music at open mics, blues jams, fusion jams, and go see my peers play. I knew it was important to be seen on the scene.

RANDOM AXIS

During those years in Dallas, my Hunger shifted from academic Skill development and training toward trying to get consistent paid gigs. I was especially motivated to become part of a well-known local group called Random Axis.

Random Axis was *the* band in the Dallas area. Even when I was still in school, my buddy Dan—who was in the band at the time—left the drum chair, and the band had auditions to replace him. I actually said to myself, "If I can get this gig, maybe I won't go to school. I'll just work five nights a week with this awesome band!" But thank God that didn't happen, because I wouldn't have finished my Master's Degree or played in the 1 o'clock lab band.

With polite persistence I eventually landed the drum chair with Random Axis. Reality quickly slapped me in the face. Random Axis paid $80 a night for nightclubs and $180 for weddings. If you do the math, it wasn't even $30,000 a year! I was surviving, but not thriving.

I was working on my Skill set, and I was cutting my teeth, but I knew the Dallas music scene had a glass ceiling. My old teacher at UNT, Ed Soph, said, "Redmond's still in Dallas? What is he doing? Everybody else has already moved to New York, and LA, why is he *still* here?"

Random Axis was a great cover band, but the money-for-time trade-off just wasn't sustainable. I was now focused on leveraging my Skills into a career. If I wanted to make my leap into the "big time," I would have to leave Dallas.

CHAPTER 11
RHYTHM AND RAMEN
IN MUSIC CITY

NASHVILLE MAY BE FAMED FOR ITS COUNTRY
MUSIC, BUT THIS MAY WELL BE THE CAPITAL
OF ROCK-AND-ROLL MUSIC IN THE UNITED
STATES OF AMERICA.

-PAUL STANLEY OF KISS

My Nashville Travel Companion, Cha-Cha

n 1996, I was twenty-six years old. I knew leveraging my
Relationships was the best way to get out of Dallas. I
started asking people about auditions. My friend Dan

Nelson, who played saxophone in a band called Soul Tsunami, told me about an opportunity with an artist named Trisha Yearwood.

Trisha was already an established recording artist in Nashville at the time. I sent my demo tape to Trisha's bandleader Johnny Garcia (Johnny and I are friends to this day). He said, "if you can get yourself to Nashville, I'll give you an audition."

I had only one week to learn five songs, but as usual, I over-prepared and learned *all* of Trisha's songs. I did my research, I got a haircut and a new outfit, and I booked my flights to Nashville. I was ready.

The audition with Trisha went incredibly well, and the musicians were very complimentary of my playing. The job went to a drummer that lived in Nashville. Trisha's band was kind enough to connect me with an audition for a hot new artist called Deana Carter.

Again, I had only had a week to prepare, so I learned all of Deana's material, booked the flight, and came back to Nashville to audition for her.

The same thing happened at this audition! The band loved me, but the job went to a drummer that lived in Nashville. Yet again, Deana's band was nice enough to recommend me for an audition with the legendary Barbara Mandrell. I learned Barbara's music note-for-note over the course of the week, and flew back to Nashville for yet another audition.

For three weeks in a row I jetted back and forth between Dallas and Nashville, each time with my best preparation, smiles, and handshakes. Everyone enjoyed my playing, but I never got the gig. It always came down to me and the "other drummer" that already lived in Nashville.

Sometimes, I believe the Universe will nudge you in a

certain direction. My three weeks of auditions were a sign. I quickly learned that if I wanted to compete in Nashville, I would have to *live* in Nashville.

DESTINATION: NASHVILLE

I had to take that leap! I wrote down my goal and a departure date on the calendar. I gave my band two weeks' notice, packed up my one set of drums and my little black cat Cha-Cha into my pickup truck, and set out for Music City. I went boldly into the night, chasing a new dream!

The only people I knew in Nashville were the musicians I'd met during my auditions. I had no gig prospects and very little money saved. I was armed only with my Skills, my Hunger, and my Commitment to reach my goal. Things began to eventually happen for me because I had a laser focus, passion-fueled Hunger and Commitment, a single-minded, never-say-die Attitude, and full confidence in my Skills.

Desperation born from being in such a tight corner, with absolutely all of your skin in the game, makes you really, really Hungry. It ignites that spark in you to work as hard as you can, as urgently as you can, so that you do not let yourself fail. As Ed Harris's character says in the movie *Apollo 13*, "Failure is not an option." The trick, of course, is that even if you are feeling desperate, you must never show it. People can smell desperation and it's the surest way to not get the gig or close the deal.

Even though my personal situation was desperate in one way, in another way I was excited to be in such a legendary music city. I also had confidence that I could contribute to the industry. If I failed, it wouldn't be because I wasn't good enough. Once people knew who I was and what I could do, I knew that I would make it. I thought, "I'm here, Nashville! You don't know it yet, but you've been waiting for me."

COLD-CALLING

I had something to offer, but no one knew me yet. One of the first things I did was to set about letting them know. On Day One, I started cold-calling every name in the phone book that seemed as if it had *anything* to do with music. I called event planners, churches, party supply stores, DJs, and other bands. I joined the Nashville Musicians Union, and cold-called, in alphabetical order, every name in the book. My cold-calling script read, "Hello, my name is Rich Redmond! I just graduated from the University of North Texas with my Master's degree in music education, and I'd like to let you know I'm in town. I have reliable transportation and a tuxedo. I can read music and play any style. Can you use me? I have a demo tape if you would like to hear it."

Cold-calling doesn't always lead to much, but I was also armed with four hundred copies of my demo tape, *Rich Redmond: Drums and Percussion*. This demo tape featured me playing many different styles: metal, big band, Latin, Motown, fusion, classical percussion, and more.

My demo tape really highlighted my versatility, but even if I got it into the right hands, would they actually listen to it?

My persistence paid off. Paul Ross, the band leader of a very busy working band listened to my demo on a Tuesday and hired me for a good paying gig that Saturday!

I had officially CRASH!ed through the first door of my Nashville journey.

PLAYING EVERY GIG IN TOWN

I'm still grateful to Paul for giving me my first job. While I was knocking on every door and answering every "drummer wanted" ad in Nashville, I ended up in some places that could have been in the movie *Silence of the Lambs*. I showed up at more than one creepy basement, thinking "Who knows? Maybe this could turn into something," while hoping not to get murdered. I reminded myself that Bruce Springsteen, Kid Rock, and Kiss's drummers were all found by answering an ad, so I persisted!

I took every single gig that came my way, from weddings to bar mitzvahs, corporate parties, pool parties, dance halls, strip clubs . . . supermarket grand openings . . . everything. I even backed up comedians and magicians! At the end of every gig, I would ask my bandmates how my drumming affected them and how I could improve my playing. I also played in every night club in Nashville, often for tips. Ironically, many of these famous bars are right across the street from more impressive venues like the Ryman Auditorium and The Bridgestone Arena. I set my sights on playing sold out shows at those venues, and years later, I did!

JIM RILEY

A week or so after moving to Nashville, I came across a fellow North Texas alum named Jim Riley. Jim was taking

113

the starving artist thing to a whole new level. At the time he was literally sleeping in his car. I said, "Jim, this is crazy, come live with me!" I took the rear seats out of my sexy Plymouth Voyager, laid them down, and made a bed for him. He had a dog, I had Cha-Cha, and we all squeezed into a one-bedroom apartment off of Edmonson Pike in the Nippers Corner area of suburban Nashville.

Jim and I were competing for the same gigs. Together we blitzed the town, playing for tips all over Lower Broadway. Jim managed to get a steady job with country artist Mark Chesnutt fairly early on, and then quickly went on to land a gig as the bandleader for the Rascal Flatts.

With Jim Riley Backstage on the Rascal Flatts Me and My Gang *Tour, circa 2006*

I was still playing with anyone and everyone, but I hadn't yet found the gig that would help me reach my goal. Jim's success truly made me happy, but while he found his dream job quickly, I had to continue seeking opportunities by playing clubs, doing regional tours, and hustling low budget recording sessions—all while juggling day jobs. A full-time job with a major label recording artist still eluded me, but I was slowly but surely building an incredible network of people who had faith in my abilities.

Be patient, because the *process* is where we learn and grow the most. I had an amazing, 24/7 sense of urgency. I had the Skill set. I knew I could make it happen. I just needed someone to give me a chance.

CHAPTER 12
EXCEEDING EXPECTATIONS

> IT DOES NOT MATTER HOW SLOWLY YOU GO
> AS LONG AS YOU DO NOT STOP.
>
> —CONFUCIUS

With Lonnie Wilson

When someone recommends you, you should always deliver over and above expectations. My first week in Nashville, I reached out to two of the most recorded drummers in history, Lonnie Wilson and Eddie Bayers. Both were impressed with my demo tape and recommended me for some showcases and touring jobs. To express my gratitude, it was my goal to exceed expectations, play at a high level, and justify their recommendation. I wanted to make them look good!

My first two years in Nashville were rough! There was very little money coming in, no stability. Thankfully, I had the CRASH! principles to keep me going. I made it a point to celebrate every little victory. One of my first victories was with a young singer-songwriter named Rick Orozco.

RICK OROZCO

> ALWAYS BEAR IN MIND THAT YOUR OWN RESOLUTION TO SUCCESS IS MORE IMPORTANT THAN ANY OTHER ONE THING.
>
> —ABRAHAM LINCOLN

Rick Orozco

In early 1997, I ran into the original drummer for the Dixie Chicks, Tom Van Schaik. Tom was a friend of mine from the

Dallas music scene. Tom was kind enough to give me a list of people to reach out to in Nashville.

High on Tom's list was Judy Seale, who worked at a prominent management company recruiting talent for military tours. Thanks to Tom's introduction, Judy recommended me to a young, talented Mexican-American singer-songwriter from San Antonio, Texas named Rick Orozco.

I ended up playing several USO tours with Rick. The USO is an organization that provides entertainment to American military personnel overseas. We went to Hungary, Bosnia, Croatia, Sarajevo, South Korea, Iceland, Japan, etc. These are places that most people will never see, but because I made a commitment to a life of music, I was rewarded with these experiences. My time playing with Rick lasted from the latter half of 1997 into the first half of 1998, and we developed a friendship that still exists today.

Unfortunately, Rick's career didn't take off. This was my first major disappointment in Nashville. I really wanted the best for Rick, and I hoped that I could find a stable dream job like Jim Riley had. I quickly learned that getting signed to a record deal doesn't mean the record will actually be released. I also learned that even if a record was released, there was no guarantee it would be successful. I had to develop a thick skin and go back to pounding the pavement.

FAMILY SUPPORT

THE FAMILY IS ONE OF NATURE'S MASTERPIECES.

-GEORGE SANTAYANA

My Parents Stopping by Rehearsals, 2010

I'm tremendously grateful for my parents. They are the best in the world. One of my Dad's favorite sayings is "the cream always rises." He says it is a law of the universe. He knew that I was very skilled, very committed, and working my butt off, but it would just take time. He reminded me daily to be patient.

My Commitment to my craft probably comes from observing my parents' incredible work ethic. When my dad came ashore from the Navy, he knew little about accounting, but eventually found himself in charge of the financial affairs of a large company. My mom also worked tirelessly to become a nurse, a profession she enjoyed right up until seventy years of age! My parents helped me out of some tight financial situations because they saw that I was relentless and unapologetic about pursuing my dreams. I am so indebted to them.

Through the toughest times I stayed committed to my dream. The more you meet your Commitments at every level, the more people are going to believe in you, and want to support and encourage you when they can.

Never listen to that negative inner voice that says that you are not Skilled enough, not lucky enough, or don't know the right people. If you are absolutely Committed to your dream, believe in your own Skill set, work hard at developing Relationships, and wrap it all with great Attitude, then you will succeed.

Through it all, never be afraid to lean on your family, friends, and colleagues for support as you work to realize your dreams.

CHAPTER 13
HUSTLE

Kurt Allison

KURT ALLISON

One of the first people I met in Nashville was Kurt Allison. My buddy Kurt and I have been playing music together in Nashville for over twenty years. In the spring of 1997, I was performing at a place called Barbara's in world-famous Printers Alley. I was playing Stevie

Wonder's classic song "Superstition" when Kurt's dad Ken came in. Ken had a family band called the Blues Other Brothers, which played classic R&B and rock hits at the now-defunct club Mere Bulles on Second Avenue.

Ken asked me to sit in on a few songs with the band as an audition. As soon as Kurt and I hit the opening groove of "Brick House" by the *Commodores*, I knew that I had the gig! When you connect with someone through music, a friendship can form very quickly. We went on to play riverboats, nightclubs, casinos, and private parties all over the Southeast.

In 1998, Kurt and I started playing with a recording artist named Ronna Reeves, whom I'd met when I was performing with Rick Orozco on a USO tour. Ronna was making the transition from a country artist to a pop artist. As we were playing with Ronna, I was also drumming for a group signed to Giant Records called Regina Regina. One was blonde and one was brunette. Both were cute! I was relentlessly hustling and managed to play in twenty-seven bands in 1999!

Despite my intrinsic impatience and desire to move things along more quickly, I realized that my career as a musician would be a marathon and not a sprint. This is true of every business, and every vocation. There is a saying that goes: "It takes ten years to become an overnight sensation," and I totally agree. I began playing paid gigs when I was eighteen, and I turned twenty-nine the year I played with those twenty-seven bands. I'd dedicated eleven years of my life to playing and waiting for my break. I worked harder than anybody else I knew, and I paid my dues in every sense of the word.

PARTY LIKE IT'S 1999

By 1999, my reputation as a reliable drummer was growing. The buzz was: "You need to get this guy. He will learn everything, he will be there early, he will be well-prepared, he will play tight, he's cheerful and pleasant to work with, and he's not a prima donna. Oh yeah, he's also very affordable."

Remember my original plan? Part of that plan was to travel the world on someone else's dime and see myself on television, and that was coming true.

In 1999, I got a gig with Susan Ashton, an award-winning country Christian recording artist who was managed by Garth Brooks' team. We traveled to Los Angeles to film *The Donny and Marie Show* and Austin to film *Austin City Limits*. I was very excited as this was my first taste of performing on a nationally syndicated television show.

Pat and Ida Paradiso, My Grandparents

I was eager to share this news with my grandmother. I said, "Gram, I played on *Donny and Marie* and on *Austin City Limits*! This is fantastic, this is big news!" She replied, "Yes, that's nice Richie, but when are you going to get a real job?" That was a real blow to my ego, and I never forgot it. But instead of letting it pull me down, I used it as inspiration to fuel all of my successes since. I think my grandmother Ida would be proud of me all of these years later.

My Grandparents, a Lifetime of Commitment

While working with Susan, I started playing with a recording artist on Hollywood Records named Big Kenny. That experience was lean and mean—touring low budget in a van. We played at the world-famous Troubadour in Los Angeles, and the very next day I played on *The Donny and Marie Show* with Susan Ashton.

I was far from done paying my dues, but at least it felt like someone was looking out for me and giving me the chance to market my product: me.

Most of those bands I worked with in 1999 failed, but in the end, I still remained. I had grown my network of people who had faith in my career, I'd worked hard, and I had made a better version of myself through my experiences. Hustle is never a waste of time.

CHAPTER 14
CONNECTIONS

The Three Kings: Me, Kurt Allison, and Tully Kennedy on the
Tonight Show, *circa 2009*

Another big break happened for me in 1999 when I got a gig with Pam Tillis. By 1999, Pam had an impressive body of work and a very loyal fan base. Everyone in the audience knew all the words to her songs. This was another first for me! It was also the first time I was paid a year-round salary and someone else set up my drums! Score!

The Pam Tillis gig is the only job in my career that I've gotten from an audition. Pam's team auditioned thirty drummers, but I came highly recommended from a respected pro named Jim White. I had known Jim from the University of North Texas. Even though I had to do the audition, the process was more or less a formality. Because of Jim's recommendation—built through our Relationship and strengthened by my Commitment, Attitude, and Skills—I was already the guy everyone else had to beat.

Working with Pam gave me the opportunity to really deliver. It was the first time I was under the hot lights with a celebrity's name on the marquee. It was also a great opportunity for me to continue my Skill development. Pam was very meticulous about musical elements like styles, dynamics, tempos, and fills. Working with Pam taught me to become even better at taking direction and keeping a positive Attitude while being closely scrutinized. If you have the good fortune to work with someone who demands your utmost, revel in that experience, because it will make you better. People that demand the best from others usually demand the best from themselves. We should actively seek out these situations because the experience will enhance and grow our professional Skills.

TULLY KENNEDY

While I was working with Pam, I met a bass player named Tully Kennedy. Tully and Kurt Allison were playing a gig with a singer named Aimee Johns at a club called Kickers in Clarksville, Tennessee. Aimee needed a drummer for her gig, so Kurt recommended me.

Tully Kennedy

To this day, Tully tells the story of how the doors to Kickers burst open, the sun beaming in behind me like a gunslinger in an old Western. I strutted in, overly excited to be there, hauling my dolly with my drum cases stacked high, each case neatly stenciled in bold letters: **RICH REDMOND**.

According to Tully, I swaggered in with the almost laughable excitement and positive Attitude that would eventually lead me to Madison Square Garden . . . but this was *not* Madison Square Garden. It was a strip-mall honkytonk. (Laughs).

My Cases—Still Stenciled in Bold Letters

I learned sixty songs overnight and played them with extreme confidence. Kurt winked at me and Tully fell in love with my drumming. This is a lesson in *always* doing your best work. You never know who will be watching and who will take notice and tell others. You can never "mail in" preparation for a performance. Tully loved how I over-prepared. I didn't base my preparation on the size of the job; I prepared for a career-defining opportunity. I treated every gig that way, and I kept an "anything can happen" Attitude.

With Michael Knox, 2015

Tully's uncle had a songwriting deal with Warner Chappell music. He knew Michael Knox, who was the VP of the company at that time. Michael was also the producer for a new artist named Jason Aldean, whom he had met at a talent show in Macon, Georgia. Jason had a recording deal with Capitol Records and needed a reliable band to rehearse with. Tully's uncle recommended that Tully be put in charge of finding players.

Kurt recommended me to Tully for the gig at Kickers, and I impressed Tully with my Attitude and preparation. When it came time for Tully to put together the band for Jason Aldean, he immediately thought of me. If I hadn't taken the job at Kickers seriously and put my heart and soul into it, I would have missed out on a life-altering and career-defining opportunity.

Right away, we began doing showcases, demos, and some preliminary touring. That was nearly twenty years ago, and we've been together ever since.

CHAPTER 15
TIM RUSHLOW

Rushlow Playing on the U.S.S. John F. Kennedy, 2003

The period between 1999 and 2004 was a very exciting time for me. I was simultaneously playing with Jason Aldean and Pam Tillis. To make things more interesting, another opportunity came along with an artist named Tim Rushlow.

Tim was the former front man for Little Texas, a successful recording act that had sold ten million records. Tim had a new solo deal on Atlantic Records and needed a top-notch band. Once again, Kurt and Tully recommended me for the drum chair. Relationships in action!

The Pam Tillis job was safe and stable. It was the most money I'd made in the music business to date. The one drawback was that I wasn't as close with any of the other members of her band. However, I was forming a very close friendship with Kurt and Tully, and we all knew we had something special.

I made the choice to forego stability in order to create a future for myself with my new best friends. Playing with Kurt and Tully always felt right; it was magic. I encourage you to seek out those kinds of Relationships in your life. If you surround yourself with people who have integrity, energy, and intelligence, there will be no limits to what you accomplish—even if it seems like a risk at first.

You can't get around taking risks in life. You just can't. You have to follow your gut, dig deep, and work hard. Sometimes you will fail. Failure hurts. But it hurts less when you are able to lean on your friends for support, and every failure is an opportunity to learn and grow.

FAILING UP

THE PATH TO MOMENTS OF GREATNESS IN YOUR LIFE WILL BE PAVED, IN PART, WITH SPECTACULAR FAILURES.

-LESLIE ODOM JR.

Tim's solo record deal grew into the formation of a group signed to Lyric Street Records called *Rushlow*. The first step was to record our debut record. At the time, the culture of Nashville drew a very defined line in the sand: you were either a touring musician or a recording musician, but never both. I never subscribed to this limiting belief. I made it my goal to pursue both! Producer Jeff Balding was impressed with the band's musicianship and provided the opportunity for us to do both on Rushlow's debut record *Right Now*. Jeff created an encouraging atmosphere to capture the personality of my drumming in the recording studio.

Rushlow's Right Now *Album Cover*

Meanwhile on the road, we played small rock clubs, county fairs, state fairs, and festivals. We would do press at six in the morning, play on the air at several radio stations, do sound checks, and play shows late into the evening. I was having a great time playing in the band even though I wasn't completely happy with the business structure we had set up. As hard as we were working, there wasn't a lot of money coming in. The majority of the shows we played were freebies. Young bands will often agree to play free shows in return for radio spins.

After having experienced financial stability with Pam Tillis, I was right back to eating tuna out of the can and stale pretzels dipped in mustard. I was once again on a lower loop of the music business roller coaster.

What we lacked in financial security, however, we made up for in one-of-a-kind experiences. We traveled to the farthest reaches of the world to entertain the US military. Our music was forever captured on a record that was available across the country in major stores. We made music videos and mingled with cute actresses. One day, driving down Highway 65 with Kurt and Tully in the car, we heard our single "I Can't Be Your Friend Anymore" on the radio for the first time. Three grown men broke down in tears because one of their life goals had come to fruition!

These are powerful moments that are important to feel, embrace, enjoy, and remember.

After we released two radio singles and put in a lot of hard work to build a memorable brand, we reached a tipping point and the band broke up. Kurt, Tully, and I dusted ourselves off and immediately went back to work with Jason Aldean.

CHAPTER 16
JASON ALDEAN

I DIDN'T WANT MY RECORDS TO SOUND LIKE ANYBODY
ELSE, AND WHEN I'VE GOT MY GUYS IN THE STUDIO, I
HAVE A LANGUAGE WITH THOSE GUYS BECAUSE WE WORK
TOGETHER EVERY DAY. A LOT OF TIMES, YOU BRING IN
OUTSIDE GUYS, STUDIO PLAYERS, WHATEVER, AND
THEY'RE GREAT MUSICIANS. IT'S JUST THAT THEY DON'T
NECESSARILY PLAY THE WAY I WANT IT TO BE PLAYED.
                                    - JASON ALDEAN

With Jason Aldean on the My Kind of Party *Tour*

The first thing I noticed about Jason was his amazing voice. As opposed to my university training, Aldean was a student from the school of hard knocks. His dad showed him a couple of chords on the guitar, and he immediately joined a band called *Young Guns* in Macon, Georgia. The young Jason Aldean patterned himself after Tracy Lawrence, Garth Brooks, Alabama, and eighties rockers. This young man had a quality that Michael Knox noticed right away, and decided to invest in. Aldean's voice was unique!

The music business has never been an easy thing to break into. Those first years with Jason were an endless stream of showcases for record labels. We experimented with a never-ending combination of instrumentation and imaging to find what would magically resonate with the gatekeepers and power brokers of the Nashville music scene. Those early showcases featured songs like, "Why?" "Johnny Cash," "Hicktown," and "Amarillo Sky," all of which went on to be chart-topping hits.

Producer Michael Knox was relentless in his belief in Jason and in the band. He kept us united in a common goal. Every time we heard a "no," he had us right back to trying something new. Michael knew how important it was to build a reliable and supportive team around Jason that could develop and grow together.

We kept doing showcases, and the team's persistence paid off when Jason was signed to Benny Brown's Broken Bow label in 2004.

FROM "HICKTOWN" TO "SHE'S COUNTRY"

On a shoestring budget, we cut a record that produced a breakthrough single that fought its way up the charts over the course of a year. That song was called "Hicktown."

Our close-knit "band of brothers" was out on the road.

Kurt, Tully, and my experience with Rushlow allowed us to leverage our contacts to help build Jason's career. The contacts and Relationships we'd formed with radio gave us an edge in a very important part of cultivating a rock-solid brand in country music.

The Historic Hanford Fox Theatre in Hanford, California

We played every bar and music venue in the country. We toured in a van first, and then in a second-hand bus, showering at YMCAs and nibbling on backstage deli trays for years. We opened for every *other* band in the business, like Toby Keith, Keith Urban, Tim McGraw and many more, with smiles on our faces. We also did several tours opening for the Rascal Flatts. At first, we only had an eighteen-minute set—about four songs—but that soon became a forty-five-minute slot, and then an hour.

By the time 2009 rolled around, we released the *My Kind of Party* record which included the songs "Big Green Tractor" and "She's Country." That was the tipping point!

Non-Stop Travel: From Plane to Bus

The van that led to the broken-down bus grew into multiple buses and semi-trucks moving band, crew, and gear down the highway like a rock n' roll carnival.

My Mobile Office: Ready to Rock on the Big Stage

We had built up a fan base one performance at a time and eventually Jason started headlining.

Headlining the Georgia Theatre in Athens, Georgia

All of this happened because of the collective Hunger and hard work of a team of people, on stage and off. *Everyone* was Hungry.

A ONCE-IN-A-LIFETIME COMBINATION

I am writing this book in 2018, and at this point we have done fourteen years of nonstop touring. We have recorded a body of work that spans eight albums. The Relationships forged in 1999 created the nucleus of our team and cemented a friendship that would lead to success at the highest level. In 2010, we added Jack Sizemore on second electric guitar and background vocals, and Jay Jackson on steel guitar and background vocals. It took a long time to get here, but we now have a once-in-a-lifetime combination of personalities and talent.

Kurt Allison, Tully Kennedy, Me, Jay Jackson, and Jack Sizemore at the Number One Party for "Dirt Road Anthem."

Jason's strength as an artist is the character of his voice; it's instantly recognizable on the radio. More than that, the consistency in his performance is remarkable. He sings well every night, and he has never cancelled a show.

We have a Commitment to our fans. We honor and cherish our Relationship with them, and use our Skills to give an amazing performance served up with Attitude, because we have a Hunger for excellence.

I'm very glad that I stuck it out through the hard times— that we all stuck it out. If Jason, Kurt, Tully, and I hadn't endured those lean years in Nashville and kept our Commitments to each other, we wouldn't have formed these Relationships that led to the wonderful journey we've been on together for years.

No matter what part of the journey we were in, our mindset was always to play like it was our last time ever on stage. Our sustained Commitment allowed us to develop our Skills and stay Hungry for new successes we could experience together.

CHAPTER 17
A BRAVE NEW WORLD

Sharing My Message with Future Leaders

L et's face it: the drummer has the most responsibility in the band and the most power to direct the energy and feeling of a performance. However, drummers are often overlooked in terms of recognition and glory.

The drummer is like the CEO of the band—they may not

have founded the company, but they play a huge role in cultivating the company's success. When I deliver my keynote speeches, I have the CEO of the company sit on my drum throne to get a crash course in drumming. They quickly realize what a powerful and unique job the drummer has.

In 2005, as I was using my energy to help build Jason's brand, I was simultaneously building my own as an educator. As the tour bus was racing down the highway, I called drum stores, colleges, and high schools to offer a free drum clinic.

I was close enough in age to many of the students to be approachable and fun. I had real-world music advice to offer, sprinkled in with the motivation and positivity I'd mined from my mom's self-help library. I immediately separated myself from other educators by offering useful tips for navigating the music business and life.

Speaking at the 50th Anniversary of the Percussive Arts Society International Convention, 2011

I also began to forge Relationships and write articles for *Modern Drummer* magazine, *Drum* magazine, *Rhythm* magazine, and the Percussive Arts Society's *Percussive Notes.* After appearing in the magazine many times as a writer and winning the *Modern Drummer* readers' polls as "Best Country Drummer" for 2016, 2017, and 2018, I finally appeared on the cover of the magazine for the December 2018 issue. This is something every young drummer in the world dreams of achieving!

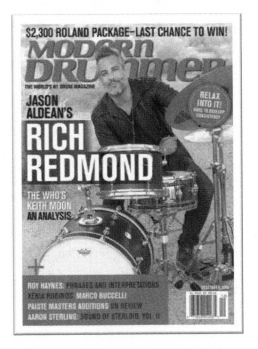

The December 2018 Cover of Modern Drummer

Developing my educational program required a huge Commitment of time and effort. I would get up in the morning to set up, tune, and clean the drums I would use that night on stage with Jason. Then, I would go set up the drums I would use for my drum shop or school event. I would then rush back to the venue and soundcheck with my band. Then I would go back to the drum shop, do the event, break down my kit, get dropped off with my drum set and unload it back into the bus, play the gig with Jason, and break down that set after the show. What a long day!

Motivating Students at Dexter Middle School, 2015

I had to do all of that work in a single day, as many times as possible on the tour, and I had no drum tech! We were playing rodeos and a lot of small towns all over the South, and I would have to clean the road dust off my drums. I was essentially running two businesses: drumming for Jason Aldean and doing my educational work as well. This was the birth of what I would call "edutainment," which is defined as offering solid educational takeaways that are wrapped up in a highly entertaining package.

My Third Annual Drummer's Weekend Nashville

Taking it one step further, I created an event called my "Drummer's Weekend." These multi-day educational events attracted drummers of all skill levels from all over the country. I hosted them in Nashville and LA for years. The community of people who have come through these camps has been amazing! The students have formed lifelong relationships, both with me and with each other. They champion their fellow campers and celebrate each other's victories in the tough as nails music business.

As busy as I was during those early days, I had very little down time on the road. In my experience, idle time on tour can be the Devil's Playground for many musicians. They get bored, seek stimulation, and get sidetracked with distractions like drugs. It's important to have something else to focus on when you're touring, and for me, that something else was teaching and speaking.

151

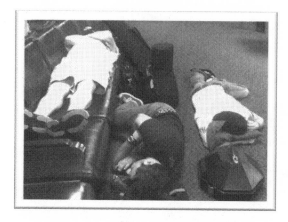

Touring is Hell on the Sleep Schedule

As time went on, I received more and more affirmation that I was offering something of value, so I began to charge money for my live events. I collected testimonials from my hosts, and I used the internet to build my brand. If you use hustle as your business model, eventually people will start to talk about you. This allows you to put a premium on what you know is a unique, quality product. My product was a business built on helping others by playing to my strengths and interests.

Whatever it is you do, these are the questions that should inform your choices:

- How do you serve others?
- Are you playing to your strengths?
- How do you continue to develop yourself?
- Are you using the free tools on the internet to build your brand?

NEW VOICE ENTERTAINMENT

*David Fanning and Jim Cooley During the New Voice
Entertainment Era*

On our days off from touring, Kurt, Tully, and I developed a reputation as a go-to rhythm section for studio recordings and showcases. A showcase is a scheduled event where an artist plays five to six songs to the "tastemakers" of the industry. Our experience, fueled by blood, sweat, tears, and miles traveled, could make even a raw artist seem incredibly seasoned. The publishers and labels in Nashville took notice of this. We were busy all of the time bringing people's music to life. After we met a young artist named David Fanning, we decided to create a new music production company called New Voice Entertainment. We produced music and procured record deals for Kristy Lee Cook, Lindsay Ell, and many others. However, our greatest success was producing two number one singles for the group Thompson Square and one for the group Parmalee.

The New Voice Production Team (Jim Cooley, David Fanning,
Tully Kennedy, Me, and Kurt Allison), with Artist Kristy Lee Cook

For ten years, we cultivated a solid reputation as a top-call production company in Nashville. In fact, we were the only rhythm section production team in the history of Nashville. Not bad. Always try to be first on the scene!

The Three Kings in Action

RHYTHM AND LYRICS

One day, a publisher named Mila Mason, who had been a recording artist in the late nineties, called me up and said, "Hey Rich, I keep seeing your name on the pitch sheet." The pitch sheet is a list of all the producers that are looking for songs to record with the artists they are producing. Mila asked if I would like to write some songs with one of her artists named Adam Fears.

I'd never thought of myself as a songwriter, but in the spirit of bravery and boldness, I said yes! I had no idea that agreeing to that one writing session would change the course of my life for the next four years.

I suggested to Kurt and Tully that we could make more efficient use of our time when we were in Nashville, and could potentially make a lot of money writing songs.

This revelation lit a fire under them, which led to Tully negotiating a four-year writing deal for us with Magic Mustang Publishing.

Signing My Publishing Deal

For that four-year period, I spent several days a week working on my new Skill set: writing songs. At that point, I had surely played on thousands of songs as a drummer, but actually writing songs was a whole new experience that taught me more about the art of storytelling though words and music.

Along the way, I met a group from Australia (actually, Tasmania) called The Wolfe Brothers. We developed a mutual respect and appreciation for each other's work and I began to write songs with them. Thanks to that Relationship, they've recorded five of my songs, three of which have become number one hits in Australia.

In the process I have written songs with:

Steve Diamond	Rebecca Lynn Howard	Jace Everett
Clay Mills	Elisha Hoffman	JT Hodges
James Slater	John Eddie	Black Stone Cherry
Michael Dulaney	Jeremy Popoff	Randy Montana
Emily West	Phil Barton	Shane Minor
Jon Nite	Jason Matthews	Ken Johnson
The Wolfe Brothers	David Cook	Kevin Kadish
Kyle Jacobs	Colt Ford	Ben Caver

...and many others.

By learning about songwriting, I became a better musician, producer, and educator. Be brave and be bold!

CRASH! AND COMPROMISE

In 2005, while performing two hundred shows on the road with Jason Aldean, I still hustled recording sessions in Nashville during the week. A producer friend asked me to record some drum tracks for an out-of-town artist named Cindy Kaza. We recorded twelve songs at Quad Studios in Nashville. As soon as Cindy and I met, sparks flew. There was an immediate attraction. After the session, Cindy and I kept in touch. In 2007, she moved to Nashville, and we fell in love.

Cindy's original interest was to become a recording artist, but after seeing the realities of the music business firsthand, she changed her mind. She went to school to become a hairdresser and then a science major before settling on her current career path. Meanwhile, I continued to perform, teach clinics, freelance as a session drummer, write songs, and produce records. We got married in 2009, and as our marriage evolved, it became more and more clear that we were moving in very different directions.

We quickly learned that you can't have everything. Given how over-scheduled I was, and how Cindy's interests began to diverge away from music, it was very difficult for our respective Commitments to each other to remain in place. Like a career, a marriage is a marathon, not a sprint. The chemistry of attraction, which Cindy and I initially had, could only take us so far. Ultimately, we were divorced in 2016.

I was always committed to the ideals of marriage: loyalty, honesty, and open communication, but the entertainment business is not for the faint of heart. Collectively, my band has missed births, funerals, weddings, graduations, and countless special occasions. The members of a band see each other more than their spouses and blood relatives. It takes a certain type of person to take on those kinds of challenges in a marriage. I would imagine it's the same for marriages with doctors, firemen, police officers, pilots, or anyone who has a demanding schedule with long hours away from home.

I do believe it's possible to have Commitment to a career *and* a marriage. However, to make things work, both partners need to be very intentional and clear about their expectations. It would be best to work this all out *before* you tie the knot, but there are times when you might not truly understand the realities of what you've committed to until you live that Commitment.

It is important to continue to reframe your Commitment as situations in life change, and to keep applying the CRASH! methods to find balance in your Relationship. You can't always have it all.

SHOUTING FROM THE MOUNTAINTOP

My goal is always to be of value and service to the world, and that is something we should all aspire to. If you have something different and special to share, then you have a responsibility to broadcast that expertise so that people can access it. If you don't share your abilities and knowledge, then you are depriving the world of something valuable and necessary.

From 2005 onwards, the CRASH! model has been firing on all cylinders in my life and in my career. The wealth of opportunities the Universe has given me is a clear sign that strategic hustle really pays off! Whatever field you are in, this is a strategy you can put to work for yourself immediately.

- Are you Hustling?
- Are you using every path available to develop your Skills and shout them from a mountaintop?
- If not, is there anything you could do differently?

Do everything possible to show others how to succeed, and in the process, you will too.

CHAPTER 18
A LITTLE HELP FROM MY FRIENDS

NETWORKING IS RUBBISH; HAVE FRIENDS
INSTEAD.

-STEVE WINWOOD

Hanging out with Nashville's Top Drummers. Left to Right: Tommy Harden, Eddie Bayers, Tommy Wells, Chris McHugh, Lonnie Wilson, Me, Greg Morrow.

One night my college friend Hal Bowman came to one of my drum clinics. Afterward we chatted about how we could make my events even more memorable and "sticky." Hal suggested an acronym that was easy for people to remember. He said, "what about crash?" and a few minutes later CRASH! was born. Thanks, Hal!

With Anthony Grady

One afternoon while I was on tour with Jason Aldean, I was teaching a lunch time clinic at Progressive Music in Raleigh, North Carolina. A gentleman named Anthony Grady happened to be in the very intimate audience that day. He had come to ask if my band would be interested in sporting his T-shirt line, but ended up staying to watch my entire speech. Afterwards, Anthony told me my teaching was full of universal messages that could be adapted by anyone, in any field, in any season of their lives. He recommended that I speak at a gathering for Cisco Systems. Cisco is a hugely successful company that runs about 80% of the Internet through cloud-based technology and hardware solutions.

Sharing the CRASH! Message

My being open to a new Relationship and Anthony's faith in my abilities led to eight other bookings with Cisco, including their Global Sales Experience International meeting at Caesar's Palace in Las Vegas. This was an incredible event where I spoke and performed for over eight hundred new team members from around the globe in the presence of their CEO.

After that, I began sharing my message with other companies like Hewlett Packard, Johnson and Johnson, and many others.

Public speaking is in my DNA. My band noticed that I was comfortable doing this and, on a whim, encouraged me to do a pre-show pep talk speech many years ago. That one occasion grew into a nightly ritual. Our show cannot begin without this NFL-style huddle. It's a big responsibility that keeps me on my toes and that I enjoy very much.

FUNDAMENTALS OF DRUMMING

As I've mentioned many times, relationships make the world go around, and it is so important to cultivate positive ones. Shouting from the mountaintop can help form those new Relationships. Since I was consistently putting content on social media, it was easy for an author named Michael Aubrecht to find me. His young son wanted to play the drums, but he wasn't pleased with any of the children's drumming books on the market at that time. Michael was already an experienced, published author so I felt great about us co-writing a book titled *FUNdamentals of Drumming for Kids.*

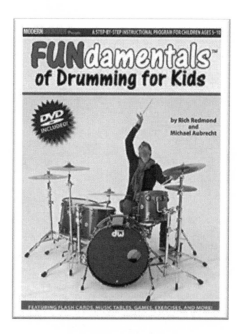

My Amazon Bestselling Book, FUNdamentals of
Drumming for Kids

FUNdamentals outlines a step-by-step program to introduce children to drumming. The book is filled with photos, coloring pages, and cutouts that keep the lessons exciting. The book includes a bonus DVD that provides a one-on-one lesson with me. We designed the book to be used by public school teachers, independent music schools and private lesson teachers alike. I am incredibly proud of the book and am indebted to the many drum teachers around the world that use it to teach new young drummers.

JIM MCCARTHY AND THE PICK RICH'S BRAIN PODCAST

With Jim McCarthy in CRASH Studio, Nashville

Social media platforms can provide an opportunity to develop Relationships with people whom you might not otherwise meet face-to-face. A great example of this is the Relationship I've had for some time now with my friend Jim

165

McCarthy. I met Jim in the early days of social media via *Myspace*. Jim is a fellow drummer, entrepreneur, and voice-over artist. At the time, I was interested in voice-over as a new Skill set and potential revenue stream. Jim and I decided to meet at the Calypso Café in Nashville, an establishment that has provided great food to starving musicians for years.

Over the years, Jim has become my muse. He is someone who not only believes in me, but who also takes the time to affirm that belief. He has always encouraged me to stay the course, stay on track, and keep doing what I'm doing. He has filmed many promotional videos for me and is now the producer for my *Pick Rich's Brain* podcast. I interview fellow drummers, musicians, actors, thought leaders, and entrepreneurs on my podcast, which is available on iTunes, Google Play, Stitcher, YouTube, and my website (www.richredmond.com).

In the spirit of a true connector, Jim is also the person who introduced me to Paul Deepan, the co-author of this very book. Once again, this illustrates the power of developing and nurturing Relationships.

JON HULL

I met my drum tech Jon Hull in a meet and greet line after my appearance at the 2011 Percussive Arts Society Convention. He took a chance and waited until the end of the line to talk to me. Jon needed an internship to complete his degree. I took a risk, and said yes. At first, he shadowed me in the studio and at local events. Then I asked him if he wanted to go out on the road and experience that side of the industry.

With Jon Hull, 2018

There were growing pains along the way, but he was eager and enthusiastic and we worked well together. I championed him to get the job as my drum tech, and it has become a life-changing experience for both of us. He has been able to go straight to the top of his field, becoming well-respected in a cut-throat industry after only seven years! In addition to our work together, Jon has worked with OAR, Young the Giant, Paramore, Story of the Year, Feluja, Alabama Shakes, Cage the Elephant, and many other top recording acts.

Jon is my onsite support for everything from CRASH! speaking engagements to TV appearances with Jason Aldean. He manages my educational events and even serves as house engineer at my CRASH recording studio in Nashville. It all started with a smile and a handshake.

We successfully cultivated a relationship that mixes friendship and business in a way that is prosperous for both of us. These kinds of risks and rewards are relevant in any kind of relationship, from romance to your career. Take a chance!

DRUMMING IN THE MODERN WORLD

Another Relationship that came through a mutual friend is with Eric Dorris, who I met through my friend Vic Salazar. Vic is a dear friend and the backbone of the Chicago music scene. He knows everyone in town and has always hosted my educational events in Chicago. Vic told me it was time to leave my mark on the world and create a legacy product. He then introduced me to Eric who helped me produce and direct *Drumming in the Modern World.*

With Victor Salazar

This video series is comprised of 120 mini-films and features over five hours of educational insight into drumming and the music business. I designed it to expand the knowledge and expertise of any drummer at any level. It was recorded at Nashville's legendary "Ronnie's Place" studio and was shot in HD. Jon Hull served as drum tech and kept the five-day production running smooth.

With Eric Dorris

Eric spent countless hours filming and editing to craft the final product. Many people have told me that this product has opened doors and inspired them to reach for new artistic levels. Mission accomplished.

Behind the scenes from Drumming in the Modern World

The best things in my life have happened through a web of friendships and Relationships that became life-changing.

CHAPTER 19
HUNGRY FOR A NEW CHALLENGE

NO MATTER HOW FAR A PERSON CAN GO, THE
HORIZON IS STILL WAY BEYOND YOU.
                        -ZORA NEALE HURSTON

Pursuing a New Craft

Whatever your dream, goal, or aspiration is, CRASH! can help get you there more surely and more reliably, by providing you a roadmap to help you control the only things you can control: your own thoughts, actions, words, and choices. I believe that when you achieve any one dream, you *must* develop a Hunger for new dreams.

Pursue those new dreams with the same Commitment to the CRASH! formula that helped you achieve your initial dream.

ACTING

One afternoon in 2013, I was teaching at the Drum Channel in Oxnard, California. My cameraman for the day was José Altonaga, who was an experienced editor, cameraman, producer, and director in Hollywood.

On set that day, José said, "I've just gotten a movie green-lit called *Reawakened*, and I want you to play the part of Lieutenant Paxton!" And I said, "Thank you, but you know I'm not an actor." José quickly replied, "You *are* an actor! You are perfect for this part!" Always open for a new, fun challenge, I immediately said yes.

I got the script, memorized my lines, got an acting coach, went shopping for my own wardrobe, and once again was over-prepared. I took what had made me successful in the world of drumming and applied that to this new opportunity. The reaction I received during the experience filming was fantastic. The other actors on set affirmed my ability and encouraged me to keep going.

A Still Frame from Reawakened

My philosophy is, if you are going to do something: GO BIG! Jump into the deep end of the shark-infested pool. Anything you want in life is on the other side of that pool. It won't be easy to get across, but it will be worth it.

Pursuing acting made sense to me because if you have ever watched a music video or an awards show, many times the musicians are "miming" to a pre-recorded piece of music. Isn't that acting? You better believe it is.

My journey led me to study acting in Nashville and Hollywood. I took an Improv comedy class with the Upright Citizens Brigade in Hollywood (founded by Amy Poehler). In Los Angeles, I've worked with people whose only goal in life is to act. Their Skills and Hunger push me to improve. Every day is a new day to create new Relationships that I know will pay off in the future.

With My First Acting Coach, Stephen Snyder

A fellow actor, Shawn Hawkins, recommended me to the director of a horror film called *All Light Will End*, which we shot in 2017. I played the role of an over-caffeinated radio DJ named Chris. It was totally in my wheelhouse.

Movie Poster for All Light Will End

I've produced and acted in several short films since then, including "The Jam Session," "Life in the Suburbs," "The Audition," and "A Small Big Problem." I'm also doing voice-over work. I have a manager and agents in Los

Angeles, Nashville, and Atlanta. Heck, I even auditioned two times for roles on *The Young and the Restless*, one of the longest running daytime dramas in history.

My first TV break came in the form of a job playing a cop on SYFY network's runaway hit *Happy!* I led a squad of 6 police officers and had several speaking parts. I acted all day with the lead actor Christopher Meloni. You know him from HBO's *OZ* and *Law and Order: SVU*. I learned so much and had a ball. I prepared, nailed my lines, was fully present and was able to quickly follow directions. I was swimming in the deep end of the pool with seasoned actors who pursue acting and only acting every day.

It's funny how people are always asking me about when I hope to get my big break acting. The thing is that everything I do is one more link in the chain of success. I'm not in a hurry. As long as I am committed to the craft, always putting out a consistent effort from my heart, preparing, hustling and networking . . . it will happen.

How I got that job on *Happy!* is a lesson in relationships for sure. My friend Arlis Albritton felt good enough about my skills and hustle as an actor that he connected me with Skip Williamson. Skip is not only the owner of *Revolver* magazine, but the producer of the *Underworld* movies with Kate Beckinsale.

Skip and his wife enjoy country music, so I invited them backstage at one of my gigs in the Northwest. I played bartender and we hit it off. Skip checked out my promotional materials and introduced me to his friend Brian Taylor. You know Brian as the writer and producer of the movie *Crank*.

Brian checked out my materials and booked me, sight unseen, for a small part on a show called *Happy!* that he created, wrote, produced, and directed. Wow! Everything starts with a handshake and I will always live my life by this principle.

Having a Rough Day on the Set of Reawakened

I have no idea where this new vocation might lead, but, being true to CRASH!, I'm keeping an open and positive Attitude to all possibilities. After being a member of someone else's team for so many years, it's nice to have people that are on my team. I let these people know on a regular basis how much I appreciate them. Who's on your team? Let them know how special they are and how much of a difference they make in your company and in your life!

Acting may seem like a big leap, but everything I've done has grown organically from something I was already doing. It's not like I decided to become a phlebotomist or go to culinary school!

Drumming grew into teaching, then speaking, and then acting, hosting, and voice over work. Yes . . . voice over work. I took classes, created a demo, and got my Skill set together so I could do things like expertly record the audio version of this very book.

Leverage *your* Skill set! This works for any business or life pursuit that you can imagine. If you use your Skills to the best of your ability, then you will find other avenues for expression, *new* Skills to develop, or even a new and exciting vocation.

SURROUND YOURSELF WITH TALENT

In 2018, I formed a company called 1225 Entertainment with my partner Mike Krompass. Mike is an insanely talented individual. He plays drums, bass, electric guitar, acoustic guitar, and keyboards; sings; produces music; and is a top-notch businessman with tons of real-world savvy. He is a perfect match for my energy and ambition.

I tend to be on the front lines all the time, traveling and meeting new people constantly. My role in the organization is to find new talent, develop business, and also handle social media for our recording acts. I partnered with Mike because he has so many skillsets that I don't have, and together we are lethal. Find the people that complement your Skills and create synergy. You can get way more done by celebrating your strengths than trying to fix the chinks in your armor.

The 1225 Entertainment Logo

In the short time 1225 Entertainment has been in business, we have started a record label, created a side project rock band called *The Fell* (with rock bass legend Billy Sheehan), and produced great talent like Billy Ray Cyrus, Steve Harwell of Smashmouth, and many others. We are literally just getting started. There is strength in numbers. I will go to my grave living by this principle.

CHAPTER 20
REMEMBER THIS!

THIS ABOVE ALL; TO THINE OWN SELF BE
TRUE.

-WILLIAM SHAKESPEARE

On the night of Sunday, October 1, 2017, Jason, Tully, Kurt, Jack, Jay, and I, along with a sixty-person crew, were performing on stage at the Route 91 Harvest Music Festival on the Las Vegas Strip in Nevada. Without warning, a gunman opened fire on our crowd of 22,000 concertgoers, causing a general panic. Between 10:05 and 10:15 p.m. local time, a sixty-four-year-old man named Stephen Paddock fired over 1,100 rounds from his suite on the thirty-second floor of the nearby Mandalay Bay hotel, killing fifty-eight people and injuring 546 others. An hour after Paddock fired his last bullet, he was found dead in his room from a self-inflicted gunshot wound. His motive remains unknown.

Two Songs Before the Shooting in Vegas

The following Saturday, October 7th, we performed the Tom Petty tune, "I Won't Back Down" on the iconic TV show, *Saturday Night Live*. This song was a tribute to the people who were killed or injured in Vegas and their families.

The *Saturday Night Live* Performance

During the week, I received countless messages of support (as did all the members of Team Aldean) from so many people that I've met over the course of my life. Even celebrities like Bono reached out to us to let us know they were thinking of us. The *SNL* performance was a powerful and sobering experience. Two weeks later, we resumed Jason's 2017 tour. This was a testament to our Commitment to our ultimate purpose: bringing music to the fans.

I know in my heart of hearts that my survival was a gift from the heavens. I have so much more work to do in the world. I know I can make a difference through education, entertainment, and motivation. I don't take this gift for granted.

Commit to your dreams and goals, build authentic Relationships, maintain a positive Attitude, master the Skills needed in your chosen field, and always stay Hungry to improve.

Here's to *Your* Success!

STAY IN TOUCH

I hope you enjoyed this book. Please feel free to keep in touch with me. If you have questions about anything at all, please feel free to email me: theredmond@gmail.com.

You can also find me online:

www.richredmond.com
www.crashcourseforsuccess.com
www.drumminginthemodernworld.com
www.richacts.com
www.imdb.me/richredmond
www.youtube.com/richredmond
www.vimeo.com/richredmond

Facebook:@richredmond
Instagram:@richredmond
Twitter:@richredmond
LinkedIn: @richgrooveboyredmond

Listen to the #PickRichsBrain podcast on Stitcher, Google Play, iTunes, and on my website.

To book me, email: Booking@richredmond.com.

ABOUT THE AUTHORS

ABOUT RICH REDMOND

Rich Redmond is a top call recording drummer/percussionist based in Nashville and Los Angeles. Rich's versatile, dynamic, and rock-solid drumming is the sound behind many of today's top talents. Rich has toured/recorded/performed with: Jason Aldean, Garth Brooks, Ludacris, Kelly Clarkson, Bryan Adams, Bob Seger, Chris Cornell, Joe Perry, Jewel, Miranda Lambert, Luke Bryan, Keith Urban, Derek Trucks, Florida Georgia Line, Thomas Rhett, Lit, Travis Tritt, Kelly Hansen (Foreigner), Mickey Thomas (Jefferson Starship), Thompson Square, Little Big Town, Kelsea Ballerini, Steel Magnolia, Pam Tillis, Vince Gill, Susan Ashton, Deana Carter, Marty Stuart, 1,000 Horses, Chris Stapleton, Montgomery Gentry, Alabama, John Anderson, Trace Adkins, Jennifer Nettles, Sara Evans,

Darius Rucker, Kenny Rogers, Rascal Flatts, Emily West, The Pointer Sisters, Lauren Alaina, Tyler Farr, Flaco Jiminez. Brantley Gilbert, Hank Williams III, Doc Walker, Gene Watson, Mindy McCready, Richie McDonald, Andi Griggs, Jedd Hughes, Patricia Conroy, Earl Thomas Conley, Catherine Britt, Anita Cochran, Jim Brickman, John Anderson, Lila McCann, Lindsay Ell, Kristy Lee Cook, Michael Peterson, The Roadhammers, The Stellas, Rushlow, Chuck Wicks, Steve Allen, Phyllis Diller, Kid Rock, Brad Gillis, Julian Coryell, Chris Daughtry, Charles Kelley, and many others. Rich has played drums and percussion on twenty-six #1 singles with sales well over the twenty million mark. As a high-energy live showman, Rich plays sold out shows nightly in amphitheaters, arenas, and stadiums across the world, reaching over two million fans per year.

Rich has appeared multiple times on a trail of television shows such as *Saturday Night Live, The Voice, American Idol*, The Grammy Awards, *The Tonight Show* (with Leno, O'Brien, and Fallon), *The Today Show*, Conan O'Brien, Jimmy Kimmel, Craig Ferguson, *Good Morning America*, Ellen, The CMA Awards, ACM Awards, CMT Awards, and ACA Awards, as well as being prominently featured in nineteen popular music videos. Rich has produced three #1 hits for the groups Thompson Square and Parmalee. As a songwriter, Rich has celebrated three #1 songs with Australia's The Wolfe Brothers. Rich is a co-owner of 1225 Entertainment and 1225 Label Group along with partner Mike Krompass. The team is working to breathe new life into the music machinery that is Nashville.

As an international motivational speaker, Rich brings his "CRASH! Course for Success" motivational drumming event to drum shops, music stores, high schools, colleges, and corporate events across the world. Some of Rich's clients include Cisco, Johnson and Johnson, Hewlett-Packard, Microsoft, Presidio, Hard Rock Café, and many others. Rich presented at The Percussive Arts Society Convention in 2011 and 2013. Rich is an adjunct faculty member at Musician's Institute in Hollywood and The Drummer's Collective in New York City.

Rich began playing drums at age 8 and eventually played in the prestigious 1:00 Lab Band at The University of North Texas. Receiving his Master's Degree in Music Education, Rich now combines his classical training and 'street smarts' musicianship to bring his passion-filled drumming to the world.

Rich was named "Country Drummer of The Year" in *Modern Drummer Magazine* in 2015, 2016, 2017, and 2018. Rich was voted "Best Country Drummer" and "Clinician" by both *Modern Drummer* and *Drum!* Magazines for several years. Rich's first book, *FUNdamentals of Drumming for Kids Ages 5-10*, is published by *Modern Drummer* and is an Amazon bestseller.

Rich is also a columnist for *Modern Drummer*, *Drum!*, *Rhythm*, *In Tune*, and *Canadian Musician* magazines.

Rich has a signature stick from Promark called "The Rich Redmond Active Grip 595," a bass drum beater he designed with DW Drums called "The Black Sheep," and signature collectible drum cases from Humes and Berg. Rich's five-hour digital educational package is available at www.drumminginthemodernworld.com.

As an actor, Rich has appeared in films such as *Reawakened* and *All Light Will End*, and SYFY Network's hit show *Happy*.

ABOUT PAUL DEEPAN

Paul Deepan was born in Port-of-Spain, Trinidad. He has lived in Trinidad, England, and Canada, as well as the United States. Paul received his undergraduate degree in Zoology from the University of Toronto, and Master's degrees in Biology and Business Administration from the Universities of Waterloo, and Western Ontario, respectively.

Following an extended career in the pharmaceutical industry, Paul leveraged his knowledge in the life sciences and business to become an author in the areas of health care, business, and finance. He ghostwrites, co-authors, and edits book-length projects for clients while following his own creative pursuits. A CRASH! Course for Success is his fourth non-fiction book to be written in collaboration with clients. He is also the author of the award-winning fantasy novel, *The Fruit of the Dendragon Tree*.

ACKNOWLEDGMENTS

I would like to thank my parents, Richard and Patricia Redmond. You are the most loving and supportive couple ever. Fifty years and going strong! You always supported my dreams and for that I will be eternally grateful. You showed me the virtues of hard work, but more importantly, you showed me what love looks like.

To my grandparents Pat and Ida. You taught me some really important stuff! You were the shining example of how consistent hard work leads to a comfortable and happy life. You also taught me about the importance of family. I miss you.

To my brothers Jason and Michael. Thanks for putting up with the noise all those years. I love you.

To Lisa, Richie, Pam, Billy, Gary, Teri, and all of my extended family: thanks for taking me to my drum lessons and for thinking I was always on track to doing something cool. It didn't go unnoticed.

To my co-author Paul Deepan! Thanks for helping shape my story into a sexy and digestible nugget (and for the amazing home cooked meals and vino)! You are a great man. To my friend Michael Aubrecht, who originally started jotting down my story through a long series of phone interviews...thank you for your time and talent. You are such an encouraging friend.

This book could not have happened without my amazing editor Carrie Miller. Thanks for letting me ramble for hours at a time and for bringing the whole project together! You were a massive piece of this jigsaw. I owe a lot to JC Clifford and Jennifer Della'Zanna (now that's Italian) for bringing you into my life.

Thank you, Hal Bowman, for your long friendship and inspiring the birth of CRASH. You changed my life. Who knew that wearing snare drums on the 50-yard line of a football field in freezing temperatures would lead to this?

Thank you, Anthony Grady, for believing in my "mouth droppings" and bringing me into the Cisco family. You helped bring me into a new life chapter. Good job! Jim McCarthy, you are my Muse! You believe in me more than I believe in myself sometimes. Thanks for keeping me accountable and for inspiring me to stay hungry, relevant, and ever-growing. Cris Cohen, thanks for helping me use the power of social media to get my thoughts out to the world over the years.

Mary Archer and Cindy Kaza. Thanks for the lessons. We all come into each other's lives for a reason. I truly believe that in my heart.

Jason Aldean. You are an incredibly consistent and soulful performer. Thanks for having me on the ride all these years and for encouraging me to be my own artist. I don't know if you know this, but we changed the world together.

To Kurt Allison and Tully Kennedy. Hairstyles, clothing styles, girlfriends, wives, and even Presidents have all come and gone, but we are still making great music together! Now that's commitment! Traveling the world with you both has been a treat.

To Jack Sizemore and Jay Jackson: you guys are the best! It is truly a pleasure to share the stage (and our lives) together.

My friend Michael Knox for always hiring me to go crash-boom-bam-rattle-shake at Treasure Isle Studios year after year! You always believed in me and I am forever grateful.

To the entire Aldean crew and team: thank you for always bleeding excellence! It's my honor to be part of something so unique.

To Jon Hull for making my life manageable and being such a great friend. Thanks for coordinating my music education events and making my drums sound like Golden Gods. You give me that "white glove" treatment on a daily basis. I am spoiled rotten. You really are like a son to me! Thank you!

A giant thank you to all of my great teachers over the years: my first drum teacher, Jack Burgi from The Milford Percussion and Guitar Workshop in Milford, CT; Byron Mutnick, Ricky Malachi, and Jim Hargrove from El Paso, TX; Alan Shinn at Texas Tech University; and Ron Fink, Henry Okstel, Robert Schietroma, and Ed Soph at the University of North Texas. Thanks for your wisdom. I soaked up every bit of it!

I also want to thank all of the musicians from New York to Los Angeles and around the world that I have ever performed with since 1976! I learned from all of you! Thank you!

Special thanks to the music community of Nashville. WE live in a very special city. Let's never take it for granted.

Thank you to all of my friends and supporters at: DW Drums, PDP Drums, Latin Percussion, Sabian Cymbals, Promark Drumsticks, Remo Drumheads and World Percussion, Humes and Berg Cases, Roland Electronics, Drumtacs, Cymbolt, Cympad, Great Leather, Alcorn Custom Case, Rhythmtech Percussion, Grover Percussion, Drumdial, Tunebot, Big Fat Snare, Qwikstix, Danmar, Anthology Gear Wear, Woodshed Stage Art, Prologix Percussion, Auralex, Samson Technologies, Audio Technica Microphones, and Porter and Davies Drum Thrones.

Those of you that have helped me bring my message to the classroom and the board room . . . you know who you are . . . thank you!

Thank you, Eric Dorris, for capturing my passion on film and to Vic Salazar for introducing us. We have had so much fun; it should be illegal.

Thank you, Brian Dominey and Adam Silverman, for your amazing web design over the years. You are both class acts.

Thank you to all of my fans! The fact that you sometimes travel great distances to see me play, speak, or teach humbles and inspires me.

I truly believe we all come into each other's lives for special reasons. If you ever saw "something" in me and encouraged me or supported me . . . I haven't forgotten. I will never forget. I will always remember. I appreciate our time together. I seek inspiration everywhere and I'm glad you were part of my life journey. Thanks again . . . and . . . again.

Finally, thanks to YOU the reader, for taking the time to

read my book! It is my goal in life to help people. I hope that you will find many things in this book to benefit your own journey as you strive to achieve success and fulfill your dreams. I believe in you. You can do it.

Rich Redmond

PHOTO CREDITS

1 Courtesy of Jeff Cristee / 3 Author Collection / 5 Courtesy of Chris and Todd Owyoung / 9 Courtesy of Author / 10 Author Collection / 12 Courtesy of Cory Dewald / 15 Courtesy of Paul Griffin / 17 Courtesy of Jimmy Cannon / 18 Author Collection / 24 Courtesy of Jon Hull / 29 Chris and Todd Owyoung / 31 Author Collection / 32 Courtesy of Lauren Elle Jaye / 35 Courtesy of Dennis Gast / 36 Author Collection / 37 Author Collection / 39 Courtesy of Torry Pendergrass / 41 Courtesy of Chris and Todd Albion / 43 Courtesy of Alex Solca / 45 Author Collection / 48 Courtesy of Tony Barbera / 51 Courtesy of Michael Lanier / 55 Author Collection / 57 Courtesy of Cory Dewald / 60, 62 Courtesy of Lauren Elle Jaye / 63 Author Collection / 65 Author Collection / 66 Courtesy of Miguel Monroy / 67 Author Collection / 68 Courtesy of Jon Hull / 71 Author Collection / 73 Courtesy of Chris and Todd Owyoung / 75, 76, 77, 78, 79, 80, 81, 82, 84, 86, 88, 89, 91, 101, 105, 107, 112, 115 Author Collection / 116 Courtesy of Rick Orozco / 118 Author Collection / 119 Courtesy of Kurt Allison / 121, 122, 125 Author Collection / 127 Courtesy of Tully Kennedy / 128 Courtesy of Sayre Berman / 129 Courtesy of Lauren Elle Jaye / 131, 133, 135, 136, 137, 138, Author Collection / 141 Courtesy of Scott Kruse / 142 Courtesy of Jules Folletts / 144 Courtesy of Scott Kruse / 145 Courtesy of Lauren Elle Jaye / 146 Author Collection / 147, 148 Courtesy of Paul Griffin / 149, 155, 156, 157, 159, 161 Author Collection / 162 Courtesy of Jon Hull / 163 Author Collection / 165, 166 Reawakened / 167, 170 Author Collection / 173 Courtesy of Chris and Todd Owyoung / 174 Author Collection / 176 Courtesy of John Perdue / 177, 178, Courtesy of Chris and Todd Owyoung / 182 Courtesy of Paul Deepan / 183 Courtesy of Chris and Todd Owyoung.